BASEBALL RECORDS
Illustrated

ABBOT NEIL SOLOMON

BASEBALL RECORDS

Illustrated

ABBOT NEIL SOLOMON

CHARTWELL
BOOKS. INC

A FOOTNOTE PRODUCTION

Published by Chartwell Books
A Division of Book Sales, Inc.
110 Enterprise Avenue
Secaucus, New Jersey 07094

ISBN 1-55521-156-9

This book was designed and produced by
FOOTNOTE PRODUCTIONS LTD
6 Blundell Street
London N7 9BH

Art Director: Peter Bridgewater
Designer: Ian Hunt
Editorial Director: Sheila Buff

Typeset in Great Britain by
Central Southern Typesetters, Eastbourne
Manufactured in Hong Kong by
Regent Publishing Services Limited
Printed in Hong Kong by
South Sea Int'l Press Ltd.

Picture credits

KEY: *t* = top; *b* = bottom; *c* = center; *r* = right; *l* = left.

The author and publisher acknowledge with thanks that the photographs in this book were provided courtesy of the following: **Atlanta Braves,** pages 13 *br*, 15 *l*, 35 *tr*, 57 *cl*, 72 *bl*; **Baltimore Orioles** pages 11 *br*, 45 *bc*, 46 *tc*, 108 *tc*, 129 *cr*, 137 *tc*, 149 *tr*; **Boston Red Socks,** pages 6 *tr*, 9 *t*, 26 *bl*, 33 *c*, 37 *tr*, 40 *l*, 42 *tr*, 52 *tc*, 78 *c*, 79 *br*, 79 *bl*, 80 *tl*, 81, 82 *tl*, 91 *tr*, 92 *br*, 107 *cr*, 117 *tr*, 119 *cl*, 124 *br*, 129 *bl*, 137 *br*; **California Angels,** pages 41 *l*, 48 *tr*, 51 *cl*, 52 *bl*, 56 *tc*, 62 *tc*, 67 *tc*, 68 *bl*, 110 *br*, 151 *bl*; **Chicago Cubs,** pages 6 *bl*, 10 *tc*, 38 *tc*, 100 *cr*, 104 *c*, 105 *tr*, 114 *tc*, 116 *bl*, 145 *tr*, 146 *c*, 154 *tc*; **Chicago White Sox,** pages 8 *br*, 79 *tl*; **Cincinnati Reds,** pages 9 *bc*, 42 *tl*, 83 *c*, 85 *t*, 85 *br*, 92 *tc*; **Cleveland Indians,** pages 19 *br*, 20 *bl*, 33 *bl*, 50 *c*, 53 *c*, 67 *tr*, 69 *tc*, 71 *tl*, 76 *tr*, 90 *br*; **Detroit Tigers,** pages 7 *b*, 8 *bc*, 33 *tr*, 36 *c*, 58 *tc*, 60 *cr*, 133 *c*, 135 *tc*, 137 *tr*; **Hastings Collection,** pages 6 *br*, 8 *t*, 8 *bl*, 9 *bl*, 10 *bl*, 10 *br*, 11 *bl*, 12 *tc*, 12 *tr*, 12 *bc*, 12 *br*, 13 *c*, 14 *l*, 14 *r*, 16 *l*, 16 *tr*, 16 *br*, 17 *tc*, 17 *tr*, 17 *c*, 17 *bl*, 17 *br*, 18 *lc*, 18 *c*, 18 *r*,

19 *c*, 20 *tr*, 20 *br*, 21 *bl*, 23 *tc*, 23 *c*, 23 *bl*, 23 *br*, 24 *br*, 25 *tc*, 25 *tr*, 25 *br*, 25 *bl*, 26 *tr*, 26 *cl*, 26 *cr*, 26 *br*, 26 *bl*, 28 *l*, 28 *r*, 29 *bc*, 29 *l*, 31 *tl*, 31 *c*, 34, 35 *tc*, 35 *bl*, 35 *br*, 37 *tc*, 37 *c*, 37 *br*, 38 *cl*, 38 *tr*, 38 *br*, 39 *tc*, 39 *br*, 39 *bl*, 40 *r*, 42 *tc*, 43 *c*, 44 *bl*, 44 *tr*, 44 *br*, 45 *bl*, 45 *br*, 45 *tr*, 45 *cl*, 46 *br*, 46 *tr*, 47 *bl*, 47 *tr*, 47 *br*, 48 *bl*, 48 *tc*, 49, 50 *br*, 51 *tc*, 51 *tr*, 53 *tr*, 53 *br*, 53 *cl*, 54 *tr*, 54 *b*, 57 *br*, 57 *bl*, 59 *bl*, 59 *br*, 61 *tc*, 61 *tr*, 61 *br*, 62 *bl*, 63 *c*, 63 *tr*, 63 *br*, 64 *c*, 64 *br*, 64 *bl*, 65, 66 *cl*, 66 *cr*, 66 *c*, 66 *br*, 67 *br*, 68 *cl*, 69 *br*, 69 *tr*, 70 *br*, 71 *r*, 72 *tc*, 72 *tr*, 72 *c*, 73, 74 *l*, 74 *r*, 77 *r*, 89 *tr*, 89 *tc*, 89 *br*, 91 *tc*, 92 *tr*, 93 *tc*, 93 *tr*, 93 *br*, 94 *tc*, 94 *tr*, 94 *bl*, 95 *tl*, 95 *r*, 96 *c*, 96 *bc*, 96 *r*, 97 *tc*, 97 *r*, 98 *l*, 99 *cr*, 99 *bl*, 102 *bl*, 102 *tr*, 103 *tc*, 106 *tc*, 106 *tr*, 107 *c*, 107 *br*, 107 *bc*, 108 *b*, 110 *c*, 110 *cr*, 110 *bl*, 111 *tr*, 111 *br*, 111 *bl*, 112 *r*, 112 *tc*, 112 *bc*, 113 *tr*, 114 *tr*, 114 *br*, 115 *tc*, 115 *bl*, 115 *r*, 116 *c*, 117 *br*, 118 *t*, 119 *bc*, 121, 123 *t*, 123 *b*, 124 *tr*, 124 *c*, 124 *bl*, 125 *tl*, 125 *l*, 125 *bl*, 125 *bc*, 127 *l*, 127 *c*, 127 *r*, 128 *bl*, 128 *br*, 128 *tr*, 130 *bl*, 130 *tr*, 130 *cr*, 131 *c*, 131 *tr*, 131 *bl*, 132 *tr*, 132 *br*, 132 *bl*, 133 *bl*, 133 *br*, 134 *l*, 134 *r*, 135 *br*, 135 *tr*, 136 *bl*, 136 *br*, 138 *bl*, 138 *br*, 139 *cl*, 139 *bl*, 139 *br*, 140 *l*, 140 *r*, 142 *bl*, 142 *br*, 143 *cl*, 143 *bl*, 143 *br*, 143 *tr*, 145 *c*, 149 *tc*, 154 *tr*, 154 *br*, 154 *bl*, 155 *tl*, 155 *tr*, 155 *bl*, 155 *br*, 156 *tl*, 156 *tc*, 156 *tr*, 156 *bl*, 157; **Houston Astros,** pages

10 *tr*, 13 *tr*, 22 *tr*, 56 *cl*, 80 *tr*, 91 *br*, 109 *tr*, 129 *cl*, 147 *tc*; **Kansas City Royals,** pages 11 *t*, 11 *c*, 12 *bl*, 60 *c*, 104 *bl*, 116 *br*, 129 *cr*, 129 *br*, 145 *tl*, 146 *tr*, 150 *bl*; **Los Angeles Dodgers,** pages 19 *tc*, 21 *tr*, 32 *bl*, 50 *cl*, 58 *br*, 60 *br*, 97 *c*, 98 *br*, 99 *br*, 100 *tr*, 100 *tl*, 117 *c*, 118 *b*, 120 *br*, 129 *cl*, 129 *bcr*, 138 *c*, 144 *tr*, 147 *r*, 147 *tl*, 148 *bl*; **Milwaukee Brewers,** pages 6 *bc*, 51 *bl*, 68 *tc*; **Minnesota Twins,** pages 43 *bl*, 56 *bl*, 58 *bl*, 90 *bl*, 151 *tr*; **Montreal Expos,** pages 24 *tr*, 32 *tr*, 50 *bc*, 56 *c*, 56 *tr*, 60 *bl*, 80 *bc*, 104 *br*, 126 *cl*, 148 *cr*; **New York Mets,** pages 11 *bc*, 27 *tc*, 27 *bl*, 27 *br*, 50 *bl*, 100 *br*, 101 *tc*, 101 *br*, 103 *tr*, 107 *cl*, 109 *bl*, 126 *l*, 149 *tl*; **Oakland Athletics,** pages 19 *tr*, 22 *bc*, 75; **Philadelphia Phillies,** pages 7 *t*, 24 *bl*, 36 *bl*, 41 *r*, 52 *tr*, 71 *bl*, 104 *cr*, 105 *br*, 106 *br*, 109 *br*, 117 *bc*, 144 *bl*; **Pittsburgh Pirates,** pages 30, 33 *cr*, 47 *tc*, 90 *tr*, 99 *bc*, 129 *bcl*, 129 *tr*, inset, 141; **Rawlings,** pages 150 *tr*, 152 *tr*, 153 *bl*, 153 *br*; **St Louis Cardinals,** pages 105 *tc*, 137 *c*; **San Diego Padres,** pages 76 *tl*, 76 *br*, 103 *bl*, 108 *tr*, 113 *c*, 129 *r*, 147 *bl*; **San Francisco Giants,** pages 32 *tc*, 33 *br*, 77 *tl*, 79 *tr*, 148 *br*; **Seattle Mariners,** pages 101 *tr*, 120 *bl*, 149 *c*; **Texas Ran- gers,** pages 55, 62 *tr*, 76 *bl*, 120 *tr*; **To- ronto Blue Jays,** pages 6 *tc*, 15 *r*, 82 *tr*, 82 *bl*, 151 *bl*, 152 *bl*.

Contents

Most Home Runs in a Single Season

L ike Joe DiMaggio's 56-game hitting streak, nobody thought that anyone would would break Babe Ruth's single-season home-run record of 60. The Babe was a baseball legend, having shown the world the wonders of smacking a ball over the outfield fence during the 1920s. There had been other challengers, such as Willie Mays and Mickey Mantle, but they were fan favorites and never suffered from "Ruthitis". Such was not the case for Roger Maris.

In 1961, Roger Maris of the New York Yankees shattered Babe Ruth's record by hitting his 61st home run on the last day of the season. With the Yankees having already clinched the pennant, the sparse Yankee Stadium crowd crammed the right-field boxes, hoping to catch the historic ball and get the $5,000 reward being offered. In the locker room, Maris was a nervous wreck. Clumps of his blond hair were falling out from the anxiety. Hounded by the press wherever he went, Maris was the object of scorn. It seemed as if nobody wanted him to break the Babe's record. The baseball commissioner, Ford Frick, declared that if anyone broke Ruth's record, an asterisk would appear next to the entry unless it was accomplished within the 154 games of Babe Ruth's 1927 season.

So on October 1, 1961 Roger Maris crushed a Tracy Stallard fastball into the right-field seats, during the fourth inning against the Boston Red Sox. Rounding the bases, Maris knew that, even with the asterisk, he was the new Home Run King of baseball.

George Bell

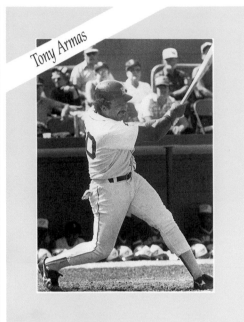

Tony Armas

Ben Oglivie

Andre Dawson

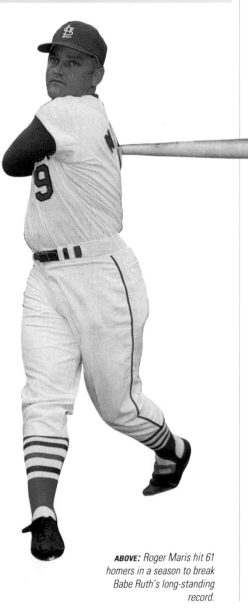

ABOVE: *Roger Maris hit 61 homers in a season to break Babe Ruth's long-standing record.*

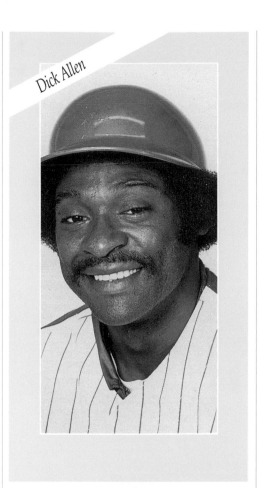

Dick Allen

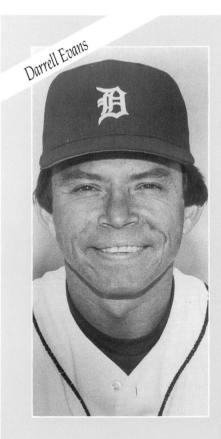

Darrell Evans

HOME RUNS IN A SINGLE SEASON
AMERICAN LEAGUE

PLAYER AND CLUB	YEAR	HR.
Roger Maris, New York	1961	61
Babe Ruth, New York	1927	60
Babe Ruth, New York	1921	59
Jimmy Foxx, Philadelphia	1932	58
Hank Greenberg, Detroit	1938	58
Babe Ruth, New York	1920	54
Babe Ruth, New York	1928	54
Mickey Mantle, New York	1961	54
Mickey Mantle, New York	1956	52
Jimmy Foxx, Boston	1938	50
Babe Ruth, New York	1930	49
Lou Gehrig, New York	1934	49
Lou Gehrig, New York	1936	49
Harmon Killebrew, Minnesota	1964	49
Frank Robinson, Baltimore	1966	49
Harmon Killebrew, Minnesota	1969	49
Mark McGwire, Oakland	1987	49
Jimmy Foxx, Philadelphia	1933	48
Harmon Killebrew, Minnesota	1962	48
Frank Howard, Washington	1969	48
Babe Ruth, New York	1926	47
Lou Gehrig, New York	1927	47
Reggie Jackson, Oakland	1969	47
George Bell, Toronto	1987	47
Babe Ruth, New York	1924	46
Babe Ruth, New York	1929	46
Lou Gehrig, New York	1931	46
Babe Ruth, New York	1931	46
Joe DiMaggio, New York	1937	46
Jim Gentile, Baltimore	1961	46
Harmon Killebrew, Minnesota	1961	46
Jim Rice, Boston	1978	46
Rocco Colavito, Detroit	1961	45
Harmon Killebrew, Minnesota	1963	45
Gorman Thomas, Milwaukee	1979	45
Jimmy Foxx, Philadelphia	1934	44
Hank Greenberg, Detroit	1946	44
Harmon Killebrew, Minnesota	1967	44
Carl Yastrzemski, Boston	1967	44
Frank Howard, Washington	1968	44
Frank Howard, Washington	1970	44
Ted Williams, Boston	1949	43
Al Rosen, Cleveland	1953	43
Tony Armas, Boston	1984	43
Hal Trosky, Cleveland	1936	42
Gus Zernial, Philadelphia	1953	42
Roy Sievers, Washington	1957	42
Mickey Mantle, New York	1958	42
Rocco Colavito, Cleveland	1959	42
Harmon Killebrew, Washington	1959	42
Dick Stuart, Boston	1963	42
Babe Ruth, New York	1923	41
Lou Gehrig, New York	1930	41
Babe Ruth, New York	1932	41
Jimmy Foxx, Boston	1936	41
Hank Greenberg, Detroit	1940	41
Rocco Colavito, Cleveland	1958	41
Norm Cash, Detroit	1961	41
Harmon Killebrew, Minnesota	1970	41
Reggie Jackson, New York	1980	41
Ben Oglivie, Milwaukee	1980	41
Hank Greenberg, Detroit	1937	40
Mickey Mantle, New York	1960	40
Rico Petrocelli, Boston	1969	40
Carl Yastrzemski, Boston	1969	40
Carl Yastrzemski, Boston	1970	40
Darrell Evans, Detroit	1985	40
Jesse Barfield, Toronto	1986	40

NATIONAL LEAGUE

PLAYER AND CLUB	YEAR	HR.
Lew Wilson, Chicago	1930	56
Ralph Kiner, Pittsburgh	1949	54
Willie Mays, San Francisco	1965	52
George Foster, Cincinnati	1977	52
Ralph Kiner, Pittsburgh	1947	51
John Mize, New York	1947	51
Willie Mays, New York	1955	51
Ted Kluszewski, Cincinatti	1954	49
Willie Mays, San Francisco	1962	49
Andre Dawson, Chicago	1987	49
Willie Stargell, Pittsburgh	1971	48
Dave Kingman, Chicago	1979	48
Mike Schmidt, Philadelphia	1980	48
Ralph Kiner, Pittsburgh	1950	47
Eddie Mathews, Milwaukee	1953	47
Ted Kluszewski, Cincinati	1955	47
Ernie Banks, Chicago	1958	47
Willie Mays, San Francisco	1964	47
Henry Aaron, Atlanta	1971	47
Eddie Mathews, Milwaukee	1959	46
Orlando Cepeda, San Francisco	1961	46
Ernie Banks, Chicago	1959	45
Henry Aaron, Milwaukee	1962	45
Willie McCovey, San Francisco	1969	45
Johnny Bench, Cincinnati	1970	45
Mike Schmidt, Philadelphia	1979	45
Ernie Banks, Chicago	1955	44
Henry Aaron, Milwaukee	1957	44
Henry Aaron, Milwaukee	1963	44
Willie McCovey, San Franscico	1963	44
Henry Aaron, Atlanta	1966	44
Henry Aaron, Atlanta	1969	44
Dale Murphy, Atlanta	1987	44
Willie Stargell, Pittsburgh	1973	44
Chuck Klein, Philadelphia	1929	43
John Mize, St. Louis	1940	43
Duke Snider, Brooklyn	1956	43
Ernie Banks, Chicago	1957	43
Davey Johnson, Atlanta	1973	43
Rogers Hornsby, St Louis	1922	42
Mel Ott, New York	1929	42
Ralph Kiner, Pittsburgh	1951	42
Duke Snider, Brooklyn	1953	42
Gil Hodges, Brooklyn	1954	42
Duke Snider, Brooklyn	1955	42
Billy Williams, Chicago	1970	42
Fred Williams, Philadelphia	1923	41
Roy Campanella, Brooklyn	1953	41
Hank Sauer, Chicago	1954	41
Willie Mays, New York	1954	41
Eddie Mathews, Milwaukee	1955	41
Ernie Banks, Chicago	1960	41
Darrell Evans, Atlanta	1973	41
Jeff Burroughs, Atlanta	1977	41
Chuck Klein, Philadelphia	1930	40
Ralph Kiner, Pittsburgh	1948	40
John Mize, New York	1948	40
Gil Hodges, Brooklyn	1951	40
Ted Kluszewski, Cincinnati	1953	40
Duke Snider, Brooklyn	1954	40
Eddie Mathews, Milwaukee	1954	40
Wally Post, Cincinnati	1955	40
Duke Snider, Brooklyn	1957	40
Henry Aaron, Milwaukee	1960	40
Willie Mays, San Francisco	1961	40
Richie Allen, Philadelphia	1966	40
Tony Perez, Cincinnati	1970	40
Johnny Bench, Cincinnati	1972	40
Henry Aaron, Atlanta	1973	40
George Foster, Cincinnati	1978	40
Mike Schmidt, Philadelphia	1983	40

Most Career Home Runs

N obody thought that Babe Ruth's record for career home runs would ever topple. Then Hammering Hank Aaron came along in 1974. For years, Aaron had been one of the premier players in the game, winning the National League home-run crown four times during his career.

Aaron's assault on the Babe's record was not without an electrifying build-up. Aaron finished the 1973 season with 713 home runs, one short of Ruth's record. So for Hank Aaron the off-season meant a barrage of reporters and interviews and the constant pressure of shattering a legend's record.

At the start of the 1974 season, Aaron didn't waste any time. On opening day, he smacked a home run to tie Babe Ruth's total. Three days later, before a packed house, Aaron drove an Al Downing pitch into the left-field bullpen for number 715 and the record. Aaron continued to play for the next two years, finally retiring with 755 blasts.

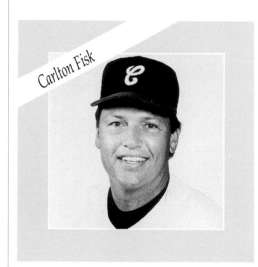

Carlton Fisk

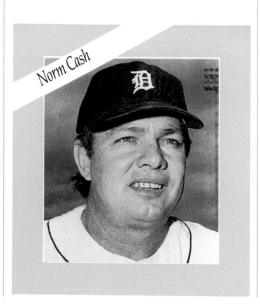

Norm Cash

MOST CAREEER HOME RUNS

PLAYER	HOMERS
Henry Aaron	755
Babe Ruth	714
Willie Mays	660
Frank Robinson	586
Harmon Killebrew	573
Reggie Jackson	563
Mickey Mantle	536
Jimmy Foxx	534
Mike Schmidt	530
Ted Williams	521
Willie McCovey	521
Eddie Mathews	512
Ernie Banks	512
Mel Ott	511
Lou Gehrig	493
Stan Musial	475
Willie Stargell	475
Carl Yastrzemski	452
Dave Kingman	442
Billy Williams	426
Duke Snider	407
Al Kaline	399
Johnny Bench	389
Graig Nettles	389
Frank Howard	382
Darrell Evans	381
Orlando Cepeda	379
Tony Perez	379
Norm Cash	377
Rocco Colavito	374
Gil Hodges	370
Ralph Kiner	369
Joe DiMaggio	361
Johnny Mize	359
Yogi Berra	358
Lee May	354
Richie Allen	351
Jim Rice	351
George Foster	348
Ron Santo	342
Boog Powell	339
Joe Adcock	336
Dave Winfield	332
Bobby Bonds	332
Hank Greenberg	331
Don Baylor	331
Willie Horton	325
Dwight Evans	325
Roy Sievers	318
Ron Cey	316
Reggie Smith	314
Dale Murphy	310
Al Simmons	307
Greg Luzinski	307
Eddie Murray	305
Carlton Fisk	304
Rogers Hornsby	301
Chuck Klein	300
Rusty Staub	292
Jimmy Wynn	291
Gary Carter	291
Bob Johnson	288
Hank Sauer	288
Del Ennis	288
Frank Thomas	286
Ken Boyer	282
Ted Kluszewski	279
Rudy York	277
Roger Maris	275
Steve Garvey	272
George Scott	271
Brooks Robinson	268
Joe Morgan	268
Gorman Thomas	268
Vic Wertz	266
Bobby Thomson	264
George Hendrick	259
Bob Allison	256
Vada Pinson	256
John Mayberry	255
Joe Gordon	253
Larry Doby	253
Andre Thornton	253
Joe Torre	252
Bobby Murcer	252
Fred Williams	251

ABOVE: Harmon Killebrew (right).

Career Grand Slams

J ust as the perfect game is the ideal performance for a pitcher, hitting a grand slam is the ultimate feat for a batter. A grand-slam home run is a combination of power hitting and good timing. The game situation – the bases loaded, the crowd roaring in anticipation, and the opposing pitcher nervously stalking the mound – brings out the best in certain batters. Joe Rudi, who hit a total of 179 home runs during his 16-year career in the American League, pounded out 12 grand slams!

The all-time grand slam leader is Lou Gehrig, the famed first baseman of the New York Yankees. Gehrig connected for 23 grand slams during his 17 years in the big leagues.

For some players, the grand slams came in bunches. Jim Gentile and Ernie Banks each hit five grand slams in one season! Other players, like Bobby Bonds of the 1968 San Francisco Giants, successfully launch their careers by pounding out a grand slam during their first major-league game.

For some of baseball's better-known home-run hitters, the grand slam was an elusive target. Willie Mays, who finished with 660 career home runs, and Mickey Mantle with 536, both are excluded from the top 20 all-time grand slam list.

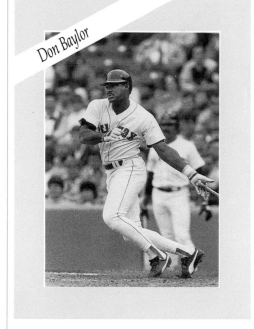

Don Baylor

George Foster

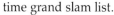

LEFT: One of the greatest ballplayers ever, Lou Gehrig hit 23 grand slams in 17 years.

CAREER GRAND SLAMS

PLAYER	GRAND SLAMS
Lou Gehrig	23
Willie McCovey	18
Jimmy Foxx	17
Ted Williams	17
Babe Ruth	16
Henry Aaron	16
Dave Kingman	16
Gil Hodges	14
Eddie Murray	14
Joe DiMaggio	13
Ralph Kiner	13
George Foster	13
Rudy York	12
Rogers Hornsby	12
Ernie Banks	12
Joe Rudi	12
Hank Greenberg	11
Harmon Killebrew	11
Willie Stargell	11
Lee May	11
Johnny Bench	11
Reggie Jackson	11
Don Baylor	11
Al Simmons	10
Vern Stephens	10
Vic Wertz	10
Joe Adcock	10
Roy Sievers	10
John Milner	10
Jeff Burroughs	10
Gary Carter	10
Yogi Berra	9
Walker Cooper	9
Sam Chapman	9
Mickey Mantle	9
Stan Musial	9
Al Rosen	9
Dick Stuart	9
Gus Zernial	9
Orlando Cepeda	9
Rico Petrocelli	9
Willie Horton	9
Rusty Staub	9
Ted Simmons	9
Ray Boone	8
Bill Dickey	8
Bob Doerr	8
Carl Furillo	8
Bob Johnson	8
George Kelly	8
Jack Jensen	8
Tony Lazzeri	8
Eddie Mathews	8
Bill Nicholson	8
Ron Northey	8
Jim Northup	8
Bobby Thomson	8
Andy Seminick	8
Norm Cash	8
Willie Mays	8
Dick McAuliffe	8
Vada Pinson	8
Billy Williams	8
Richie Allen	8
Darrell Evans	8

Most Career Home Runs by Position

P utting together the all-time home-run leaders by position yields quite an offensive lineup. Most of the players are either in or headed for the Hall of Fame. Statistics fanatics may be confused to see a total like 686 for Babe Ruth. Keep in mind that these numbers are calculated *by position*. Not reflecting total lifetime home-run production, the figures in this chart are the number of dingers hit while playing that specific position!

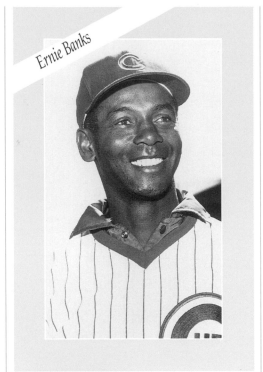

Ernie Banks

Cliff Johnson

MOST CAREER HOME RUNS BY POSITION

POSITION	PLAYER	HRS	TOTAL HRS
C	Johnny Bench	327	389
P	Wes Ferrell	36	38
1B	Lou Gehrig	493	493
2B	Joe Morgan	266	268
3B	Mike Schmidt	482	521
3B	Eddie Mathews	482	512
SS	Ernie Banks	277	512
OF	Babe Ruth	692	714
PH	Cliff Johnson	20	196

BELOW: *Joe Morgan.*

Eddie Mathews

Switch-Hit Home Runs in One Game

S witch-hitters, those batters blessed with the ability to smack baseballs from either side of the plate, are a rare commodity. Being able to switch from one side of the plate to the other means that the curveball-throwing pitcher never has the advantage.

Perhaps the greatest switch-hitter of all time was Mickey Mantle. During his playing days with the New York Yankees, Mantle led the American League in home runs four times and six times won the RBI crown. Part of Mantle's success can be attributed to his switch-hitting skills. Mantle also leads the majors in another unique distinction: he belted switch-hit homers (one from either side of the plate), during one game ten times.

Perhaps today's best switch-hitter is Eddie Murray of the Baltimore Orioles who has eight switch-hit home runs. Like Mantle, Murray is a powerful hitter who is always near the top in yearly statistics.

LEFT: Mickey Mantle may well be the greatest switch-hitter in baseball history.

SWITCH-HIT HOME RUNS IN ONE GAME

AMERICAN LEAGUE

PLAYER	TEAM	YEAR
Johnny Lucadello	STL	1940
Mickey Mantle	NY	1955
Mickey Mantle	NY	1955
Mickey Mantle	NY	1956
Mickey Mantle	NY	1956
Mickey Mantle	NY	1957
Mickey Mantle	NY	1958
Mickey Mantle	NY	1959
Mickey Mantle	NY	1961
Mickey Mantle	NY	1962
Tom Tresh	NY	1963
Tom Tresh	NY	1964
Mickey Mantle	NY	1964
Tom Tresh	NY	1965
Reggie Smith	BOS	1967
Reggie Smith	BOS	1968
Don Buford	BAL	1970
Roy White	NY	1970
Reggie Smith	BOS	1972
Reggie Smith	BOS	1973
Roy White	NY	1973
Roy White	NY	1975
Ken Henderson	CHI	1975
Roy White	NY	1977
Eddie Murray	BAL	1978
Larry Milbourne	SEA	1978
Willie Wilson	KC	1979
Eddie Murray	BAL	1979
U. L. Washington	KC	1979

NATIONAL LEAGUE

PLAYER	TEAM	YEAR
Augie Galan	CHI	1937
Jim Russell	BOS	1948
Jim Russell	BKN	1950
Red Schoendienst	STL	1951
Maury Wills	LA	1962
Ellis Burton	CHI	1963
Ellis Burton	CHI	1964
Jim Lefebvre	LA	1966
Wes Parker	LA	1966
Pete Rose	CIN	1966
Pete Rose	CIN	1967
Ted Simmons	STL	1975
Reggie Smith	STL	1975
Reggie Smith	STL	1976
Lee Mazzilli	NY	1978
Ted Simmons	STL	1979

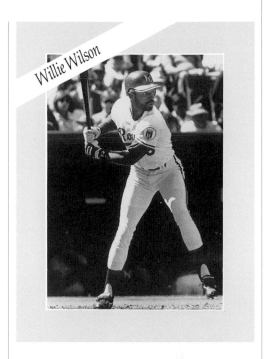

Willie Wilson

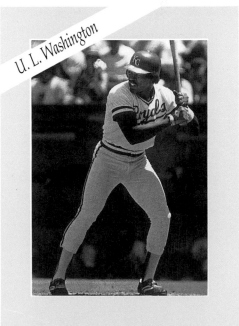

U. L. Washington

Lee Mazzilli

Don Buford

Four Home Runs in One Game

Most ballplayers average about four or five plate appearances per game. Of course, every player hopes to smack a home run every time he comes to bat. Imagine the thrill it must be to hit four homers in one game! Although some 30,000 players have suited up, only ten have hit four home runs in one regular season game.

Of the ten men in this exclusive club, only Joe Adcock of the Milwaukee Braves and Ed Delahanty of the Philadelphia Phillies hit them consecutively. Surprisingly, most of the men making this list hit their four four-baggers during an away game.

Adcock came the closest to joining a new club – the five in one game gang. After hitting his four dingers on July 31, 1954, Joe Adcock narrowly missed number five when his shot hit high off the Ebbets Field wall for a double.

FOUR HOME RUNS IN ONE GAME

AMERICAN LEAGUE

PLAYER	TEAM	DATE	INNS.
Lou Gehrig	NY	June 3, 1932	9
Pat Seerey	CHI	July 18, 1948	11
Rockey Colavito	CLE	June 10, 1959	9

NATIONAL LEAGUE

PLAYER	TEAM	DATE	INNS.
Bobby Lowe	BOS	May 30, 1894	9
Ed Delahanty	PHI	July 13, 1896	9
Chuck Klein	PHI	July 10, 1936	10
Gil Hodges	BKN	Aug. 31, 1950	9
Joe Adcock	MIL	July 31, 1954	9
Willie Mays	SF	April 30, 1961	9
Mike Schmidt	PHI	July 17, 1976	10

RIGHT: *Willie Mays.*

Lou Gehrig

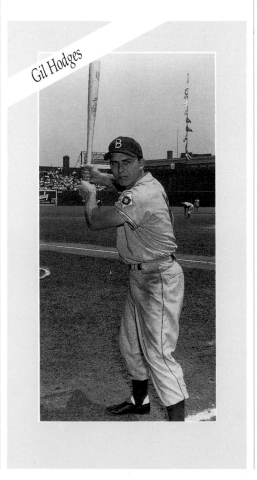

Gil Hodges

Rocky Colavito

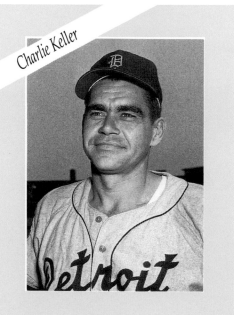

Charlie Keller

Career Multiple Home-Run Games

S ometimes it's true – when you're hot, you're hot. The hottest a batter can get is to have a multiple home-run game. Hitting a home run is such an accomplishment that getting to circle the bases two or three times during a game is a rare adventure.

Although most members of this list are well-known sluggers, a few lesser-known talents rate an entry. Along with Babe Ruth, Willie Mays, and Hank Aaron, the list includes Lee May, Gus Zernial, and Harold Trosky!

The leader of the list is the great "Bambino", Babe Ruth. During his career, Ruth had 72 multiple home-run games. He really gave those lucky fans their money's worth.

Some players, like Gary Carter and Graig Nettles, are streak hitters, who can get into that home-run groove and put a few together.

CAREER MULTIPLE HOME-RUN GAMES

PLAYER	GAMES
Babe Ruth	72
Willie Mays	63
Henry Aaron	62
Jimmie Foxx	55
Frank Robinson	54
Eddie Mathews	49
Mel Ott	49
Mickey Mantle	46
Harmon Killebrew	46
Willie McCovey	44
Lou Gehrig	43
Dave Kingman	43
Ernie Banks	42
Reggie Jackson	42
Mike Schmidt	41
Ralph Kiner	40
Stan Musial	37
Ted Williams	37
Willie Stargell	36
Joe DiMaggio	35
Hank Greenberg	35
Lee May	35
Duke Snider	34
Jim Rice	34
Rocco Colavito	32
Gus Zernial	32
Richie Allen	32
Hank Sauer	31
Billy Williams	31
Gil Hodges	30
Johnny Mize	30
Willie Horton	30
Joe Adcock	28
Chuck Klein	28
Roy Sievers	27
Lew Wilson	27
Carl Yastrzemski	27
Graig Nettles	27
Frank Howard	26
Ron Santo	26
Bob Horner	26
Roger Maris	25
Hal Trosky	25
Norm Cash	25
Gary Carter	25

Lee May

LEFT: *Babe Ruth, all-time leader in career multiple home-run games.*

Bob Horner

Most Career Leadoff Home Runs

The role of the leadoff batter in the lineup is to get on base. Usually, these players are fast-running contact hitters who also know how to take a base on balls. However, in the history of the game, a few of these leadoff hitters have distinguished themselves by being able to hit homers in that first trip to the plate.

One of the best leadoff home-run hitters was Bobby Bonds. During his career Bonds hit a total of 332 home runs. Of these dingers, 35 were hit during his first time at bat in a game. Bonds was one of those unique players gifted with power and speed. Five times in his career, Bonds had at least 30 home runs and 30 stolen bases, a major-league record.

The New York Yankees have another double threat in centerfielder Rickey Henderson. Henderson, known primarily for his record-setting stolen bases, has found the power groove. With 34 leadoff homers, Henderson is closing in on Bobby Bonds' record.

MOST CAREER LEADOFF HOME RUNS

PLAYER	LEADOFF HRs	CAREER HRs
Bobby Bonds	35	332
Rickey Henderson	34	120
Eddie Yost	28	139
Jimmy Ryan	22	118
Lou Brock	21	149
Felipe Alou	20	206
Dick McAuliffe	19	197
Eddie Joost	19	134
Hank Bauer	18	164
Tommy Harper	16	146

RIGHT: *Eddie Yost, number 3 among career leadoff home-run leaders.*

RIGHT: *Hank Bauer.*

Most Pinch-Hit Home Runs

I magine and pity the player who sits on the bench during a game, never knowing when he'll be called upon to pinch hit. Having taken batting practice hours earlier, the muscles tighten and it's difficult to get warmed up. Some players really knew how to take advantage of the situation. After getting the call, they'd grab a bat, stride up to the plate, and smack the ball over the fence for a home run.

The most productive pinch-hit home-run hitter was Cliff Johnson, who played with a number of teams, including the Yankees, the Toronto Blue Jays, and the Houston Astros. "Heathcliff" banged out 20 pinch-hit homers in his career. Also on the list are such noted pinch-hit specialists as Smokey Burgess and Jay Johnstone. Interestingly, not only does a player need to have power, but he must also be in a position to be called upon to pinch hit. Many were their team's "fourth" outfielder, who spent many innings riding the pine waiting to get into the game.

BELOW: Cliff Johnson socked 20 pinch-hit home runs during his career.

MOST PINCH-HIT HOME RUNS

PLAYER	HRs
Cliff Johnson	20
Jerry Lynch	18
Smokey Burgess	16
Bill Brown	16
Willie McCovey	16
George Crowe	14
José Morales	12
Bob Cerv	12
Joe Adcock	12
Fred Williams	11
Fred Whitfield	11
Jeff Burroughs	11
John Johnstone	11
Gus Zernial	10
Wally Post	10
Don Mincher	10
Ken McMullen	10
Mike Lum	10
John Summers	10
John Turner	10

Jeff Burroughs

Most Consecutive Games Hitting Homers Each Game

According to many statistical experts, this record is the second-greatest offensive accomplishment in the game. Ranking just below Joe DiMaggio's 56-game consecutive hitting streak, Dale Long's and Don Mattingly's marks are quite incredible. Sharing the record, each of these sluggers was able to pound out at least one home run in eight consecutive games. Long set his record in 1956; 21 years later, Mattingly equalled the mark.

Grouped in second place are six notable American Leaguers. Names like Lou Gehrig, Roger Maris and Reggie Jackson help establish the mark of six for second place. Frank Howard made the list while also setting the major league record for most home runs in six consecutive games. During his six-game streak, Howard, of the 1968 Washington Senators, drove ten baseballs over the outfield wall!

RIGHT: *Dale Long takes batting practice. It must have helped, because in 1956 he hit a home run in eight consecutive games.*

MOST CONSECUTIVE GAMES HITTING HOMERS EACH GAME

PLAYER	TEAM	GAMES	HOME RUNS	YEAR
Dale Long	Pittsburgh NL	8	8	1956
Don Mattingly	New York AL	8	8	1987
Ken Williams	St. Louis AL	6	6	1922
Lou Gehrig	New York AL	6	6	1931
Roy Sievers	Washington AL	6	6	1957
Roger Maris	New York AL	6	7	1961
Frank Howard	Washington	6	10	1968
Reggie Jackson	Baltimore AL	6	6	1976

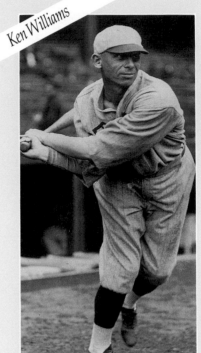

Ken Williams

Roy Sievers

Most Home Runs in Two Consecutive Games

S uperstar rookie Mark McGwire tied a major-league record during the 1987 season by crushing five home runs in two consecutive games. The figures show that the long ball is back in baseball, with record numbers of homers being hit each day.

In the history of the game, McGwire joined an elite list of 13 other major leaguers who were able to put five balls over the wall in two games. One of the game's all-time sluggers, Ralph Kiner of the Pittsburgh Pirates, accomplished the feat twice during the 1947 season. Some players make a surprise appearance on the list. Ty Cobb, who finished his career with 118 home runs, was able to bunch five of them together in 1925 during a rare power surge.

MOST HOME RUNS IN TWO CONSECUTIVE GAMES

PLAYER	TEAM	SEASON	HRs/YEAR	CAREER HRs
Cap Anson	Cubs	1884	21	96
Ty Cobb	Tigers	1925	12	118
Tony Lazzeri	Yankees	1936	14	178
Ralph Kiner (twice)	Pirates	1947	51	369
Don Mueller	Giants	1951	16	65
Stan Musial	Cardinals	1954	35	475
Joe Adcock	Braves	1954	23	336
Billy Williams	Cubs	1968	30	426
Nate Colbert	Padres	1972	38	173
Mike Schmidt	Phillies	1976	38	512
Carl Yastrzemski	Red Sox	1976	21	452
Dave Kingman	Cubs	1979	48	442
Gary Carter	Mets	1985	32	280
Mark McGwire	Athletics	1987	49	49

Ralph Kiner

Don Mueller

Cap Anson

Tony Lazzeri

LEFT: Joe Adcock.

Most Home Runs in Each Game of Doubleheader

This statistic may be a vanishing breed. With modern scheduling, the teams just don't play as many doubleheaders as they used to. In fact, most of today's doubleheaders are forced upon teams to make up for rained-out games. But in the good old days, when Sunday was doubleheader time, some sluggers must have gotten dizzy from circling the bases.

In the National League, Stan Musial and San Diego's Nate Colbert share the record of five home runs in a doubleheader, hitting at least one in each game.

The American League mark of four is shared by 12 players, including such powerhouses as Roger Maris, Jimmy Foxx, and Graig Nettles. Others, like Otto Velez and Gus Zernial, although not remembered for hitting many homers, were able to find that sweet swing during their day of glory.

MOST HOME RUNS IN EACH GAME OF A DOUBLEHEADER

AMERICAN LEAGUE

HR	PLAYER	YEAR	TEAM
4	Earl Averill	1930	Cleveland
4	Jimmy Foxx	1933	Philadelphia
4	Jim Tabor	1939	Boston
4	Gus Zernial	1950	Chicago
4	Charlie Maxwell	1959	Detroit
4	Roger Maris	1961	New York
4	Rocco Colavito	1961	Detroit
4	Harmon Killebrew	1963	Minnesota
4	Bobby Murcer	1970	New York
4	Graig Nettles	1974	New York
4	Otto Velez	1980	Toronto
4	Al Oliver	1980	Texas

NATIONAL LEAGUE

HR	PLAYER	YEAR	TEAM
5	Stan Musial	1954	St. Louis
5	Nate Colbert	1972	San Diego

BELOW: In 1954 Stan Musial spread five home runs over one doubleheader, a record matched by Nate Colbert in 1972 but never broken.

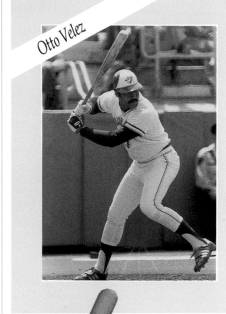

Otto Velez

LEFT: Gus Zernial.

Rocco Colavito

Major League Rookies with 30 or More Home Runs

The dream of any rookie in the major leagues is to crack the starting lineup. For some players, their entry into professional baseball comes with a bang. In the history of the game, 18 players have hit 30 or more homers during their rookie season.

Some of these rookie phenoms have gone on to illustrious careers. Among the superstar players have been Ted Williams, Tony Oliva, and Frank Robinson. Others like Hal Trosky, Walt Dropo, and Wally Berger, had lesser careers. The 1987 rookie crop produced Matt Nokes, who belted 32 homers for the Detroit Tigers and the awesome Mark McGwire of the Oakland A's, who banged out a league-leading 49 dingers. Together with other young stars like Pete Incaviglia of the Texas Rangers and José Canseco of the Oakland A's, these players thrill fans with monumental blasts into the bleachers.

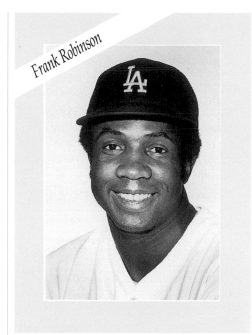

Frank Robinson

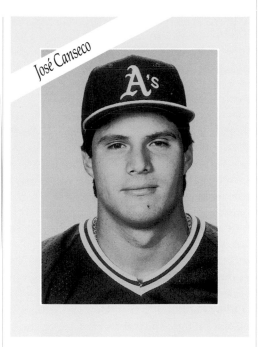

José Canseco

BELOW: Al Rosen started his long career in baseball with a bang. In 195 he set the American League record for home runs by a rookie with 37.

ABOVE: Tony Oliva (right) shown with teammates Dave Boswell (center) and Bob Allison (left).

MAJOR LEAGUE ROOKIES WITH 30 OR MORE HOME RUNS

AMERICAN LEAGUE

PLAYER	TEAM	HOME RUNS	YEAR
Al Rosen	Cleveland	37	1950
Hal Trosky	Cleveland	35	1934
Rudy York	Detroit	35	1937
Ron Kittle	Chicago	35	1983
Walt Dropo	Boston	34	1950
Jimmie Hall	Minnesota	33	1963
José Canseco	Oakland	33	1986
Tony Oliva	Minnesota	32	1964
Ted Williams	Boston	31	1939
Bob Allison	Washington	30	1959
Pete Incaviglia	Texas	30	1986
Matt Nokes	Detroit	32	1987
Mark McGwire	Oakland	49	1987

NATIONAL LEAGUE

PLAYER	TEAM	HOME RUNS	YEAR
Wally Berger	Boston	38	1930
Frank Robinson	Cincinnati	38	1956
Earl Williams	Atlanta	33	1971
Jim Hart	San Francisco	31	1964
Willie Montanez	Philadelphia	30	1971

Home Runs, First Pitch, First Major-League At-Bat

S ome players just didn't have time to enjoy the thrilling experience of their first major-league at-bat. Spending only seconds in the batter's box, they soon trotted around the bases. But can you imagine the smiles on their faces!

For these players, the first major-league pitch they saw was promptly deposited over the fence for a home run. Some of these lucky rookies, such as Bert Campaneris, went on to have memorable careers. Chuck Tanner became better known as a big-league manager.

The latest player to make the list is Jay Bell, who on September 29, 1986, made an unbelievable swing that resulted in the one home run he'll never forget.

For Brant Alyea, Ed Morgan, and Chuck Tanner, the feat was extra special. Not only did they homer on the first pitch, but they made their appearance as pinch-hitters!

Wally Moon

HOME RUNS, FIRST PITCH, FIRST MAJOR LEAGUE AT-BAT
AMERICAN LEAGUE

PLAYER	TEAM	YEAR
Earl Averill	Cleveland	1929
Ace Parker	Philadelphia	1937
Bill LeFebvre	Boston	1938
Hack Miller	Detroit	1944
Ed Pellagrini	Boston	1946
George Vico	Detroit	1949
Bob Nieman	St. Louis	1951
Bob Tillman	Boston	1962
John Kennedy	Washington	1962
Buster Narum	Baltimore	1963
Gates Brown	Detroit	1963
Bert Campaneris	Kansas City	1964
Bill Roman	Detroit	1964
Brant Alyea	Washington	1965
John Miller	New York	1966
Rick Renick	Minnesota	1968
Joe Keough	Oakland	1968
Gene Lamont	Detroit	1970
Don Rose	California	1972
Reggie Sanders	Detroit	1974
Dave Mckay	Minnesota	1975
Al Woods	Toronto	1977
Dave Machemer	California	1978
Gary Gaetti	Minnesota	1981
Andre David	Minnesota	1984
Terry Steinbach	Oakland	1986
Jay Bell	Cleveland	1986

NATIONAL LEAGUE

PLAYER	TEAM	YEAR
Bill Duggleby	Philadelphia	1898
Johnny Bates	Boston	1906
Clise Dudley	Brooklyn	1929
Gordon Slade	Brooklyn	1930
Eddie Morgan	St. Louis	1936
Ernie Koy	Brooklyn	1938
Emmett Mueller	Philadelphia	1938
Clyde Vollmer	Cincinnati	1942
Buddy Kerr	New York	1943
Whitey Lockman	New York	1945
Dan Bankhead	Brooklyn	1947
Les Layton	New York	1948
Ed Sanicki	Philadelphia	1949
Ted Tappe	Cincinnati	1950
Hoyt Wilhelm	New York	1952
Wally Moon	St. Louis	1954
Chuck Tanner	Milwaukee	1955
Bill White	New York	1956
Frank Ernaga	Chicago	1957
Don Leppert	Pittsburgh	1961
Cuno Barragan	Chicago	1961
Benny Ayala	New York	1974
John Montefusco	San Francisco	1974
Jose Sosa	Houston	1975
Johnnie LeMaster	San Francisco	1975
Carmelo Martinez	Chicago	1983
Mike Fitzgerald	New York	1983
Bill Clark	San Francisco	1986

Bill White

LEFT: Jay Bell powdered his very first pitch in the big leagues for a home run.

Most Career Home Runs in Different Major League Parks

A lmost every slugger has a favorite park. Sometimes a ballpark's peculiar dimensions are just perfect for a batter's strength. Roger Maris, for example, loved to smash the ball over the short porch in Yankee Stadium's right field. Other right-handed American League batters salivated at the sight of Boston's famous "Green Monster".

But some home-run hitters really knew how to spread the wealth. By hitting their shots in many parks, fans from all over the country got to see them circle the bases. Frank Robinson and Rusty Staub were the most benevolent players. These sluggers hit at least one home run in 32 different ballparks. Of course, it helped that they played in both leagues over their careers.

Another slugger who didn't necessarily want to favor any one park was Hank Aaron. On his way to being the all-time home-run leader, Aaron hit at least one dinger in 31 different parks.

LEFT: Frank Robinson hit at least one home run in 32 different ball parks.

BELOW: Famed as a slugger and a pinch-hitter, Rusty Staub equalled Frank Robinson's mark of at least one dinger in 32 different stadiums.

MOST CAREER HOME RUNS IN DIFFERENT MAJOR LEAGUE PARKS

HR	PLAYER	TEAMS	YEARS
32	Frank Robinson	Cincinnati NL Baltimore AL Los Angeles NL California AL Cleveland AL	1956–1957
32	Rusty Staub	Houston NL Montreal NL New York NL Detroit AL Texas AL	1963–1985
31	Hank Aaron	Milwaukee NL Atlanta NL Milwaukee AL	1954–1976 —

Home Runs in All 12 Parks in League, Season

F or the most prolific home-run hitters, every day is another shot at thrilling the fans. Since each team travels around the league, this gives the players a chance to hit in all ball parks. A few noted long-ball hitters really took advantage of the change of scenery. Seven of the game's big hitters hit at least one homer in every park during a season.

The list looks like a who's who of the big hitters during the past 20 years. In 1970, for example, the Giants' Willie McCovey, Pittsburgh's Willie Stargell, and Joe Pepitone (playing for Houston and the Cubs) each belted homers in every National League park. In 1972, Johnny Bench added his name to the roster. Five years later, another Cincinnati Red, George Foster, clobbered one in every ball park. Then in 1979, Mike Schmidt of the Phillies completed the cycle.

In the American League only Reggie Jackson, playing for the Oakland Athletics in 1975, was able to belt a home run in every park.

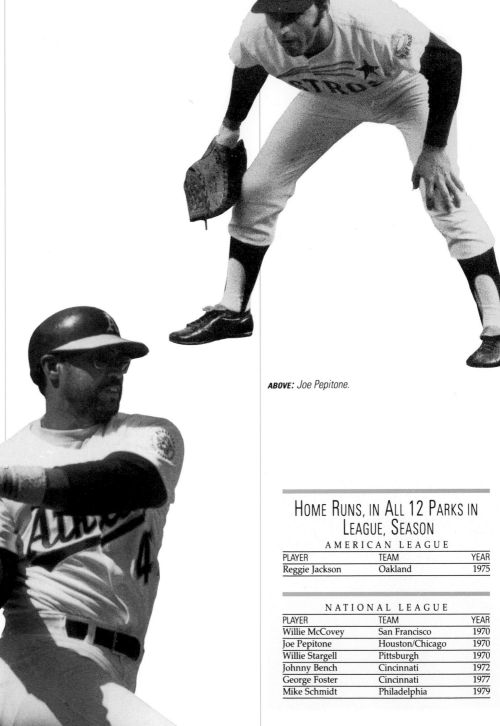

ABOVE: *Joe Pepitone.*

RIGHT: *Reggie Jackson is the only American League player to hit a home run in all twelve parks in the league in one season.*

HOME RUNS, IN ALL 12 PARKS IN LEAGUE, SEASON

AMERICAN LEAGUE

PLAYER	TEAM	YEAR
Reggie Jackson	Oakland	1975

NATIONAL LEAGUE

PLAYER	TEAM	YEAR
Willie McCovey	San Francisco	1970
Joe Pepitone	Houston/Chicago	1970
Willie Stargell	Pittsburgh	1970
Johnny Bench	Cincinnati	1972
George Foster	Cincinnati	1977
Mike Schmidt	Philadelphia	1979

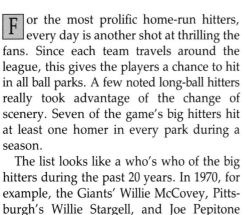

Favorite Home Run Parks

Nearly every ballplayer has a favorite park to hit in. Some stadiums are better suited for their type of swing, or some parks just feel lucky. For whatever reason, some of the games greatest home-run sluggers have hit more four-baggers in one park than another. Of course, most of these superstars hit their blasts in their home field, but regardless, they still knew how to rocket one out!

Mel Ott of the New York Giants hit 323 of his career 511 home runs at the Polo Grounds. Surprisingly, Babe Ruth was not such a selective batter. The Babe smacked only 259 of his 714 homers at Yankee Stadium. Ruth spread them around, breaking the hearts of home-team crowds all over the American League.

FAVORITE HOME RUN PARKS

PLAYER	HRs	PARK
Mel Ott	323	Polo Grounds
Ernie Banks	290	Wrigley Field
Mickey Mantle	266	Yankee Stadium
Babe Ruth	259	Yankee Stadium
Lou Gehrig	251	Yankee Stadium
Ted Williams	248	Fenway Park
Mike Schmidt	242	Veterans Stadium
Carl Yastrzemski	237	Fenway Park
Billy Williams	231	Wrigley Field
Ron Santo	212	Wrigley Field

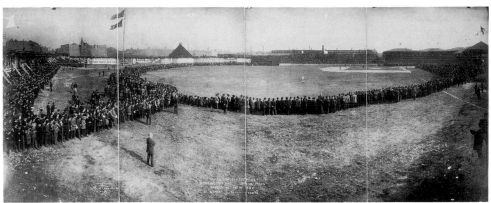

ABOVE: Where the American League played baseball in Boston in 1904 – no Green Monster here

ABOVE: The original Polo Grounds in New York City as it appeared in 1887.

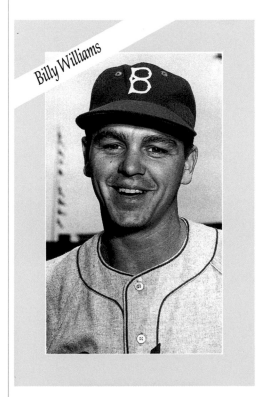

ABOVE: Hall of Famer member Billy Williams hit 231 home runs in Wrigley Field.

ABOVE: Ernie Banks loved to hit in Wrigley Field – he socked 290 homers there.

Two Home Runs in One Inning

S ome home-run hitters barely have time to catch their breath. If a team gets a hot inning and bats around, players get a second shot at the plate. A rare feat is when a player gets two hits in one inning. Even rarer are those players who have hit two home runs in the same inning. It takes not only the power to belt one out of the park, but the support the team must give by scoring runs and giving the batter a second chance. Then the opposing manager must choose to pitch to the batter instead of giving him an intentional walk.

Since 1900, 18 players have hit two homers in the same inning. While some of the names, like Willie McCovey and Al Kaline, are recognizable, others have quickly faded from memory. Sid Gordon, John Boccabella, and Rich Reichardt all had their moment in the sun.

The last player to hit two homers in one inning was Von Hayes. On June 11, 1985, Hayes thrilled Phillies fans by circling the bases twice during his first inning at bat.

TWO HOME RUNS IN ONE INNING
AMERICAN LEAGUE

PLAYER	TEAM	YEAR
Ken Williams	St. Louis	1922
Bill Regan	Boston	1928
Joe DiMaggio	New York	1936
Al Kaline	Detroit	1955
Jim Lemon	Washington	1959
Joe Pepitone	New York	1962
Rick Reichardt	California	1966
Cliff Johnson	New York	1977

NATIONAL LEAGUE

PLAYER	TEAM	YEAR
Hack Wilson	New York	1925
Hank Leiber	New York	1935
Andy Seminick	Philadelphia	1949
Sid Gordon	New York	1949
Willie McCovey	San Francisco	1973
John Boccabella	Montreal	1973
Lee May	Houston	1974
Andre Dawson	Montreal	1978
Ray Knight	Cincinnati	1980
Von Hayes	Philadelphia	1985

John Boccabella

RIGHT: Joe DiMaggio powered two home runs in one inning in 1936 making him third on the all-time American League list.

Triple Crown Winners

O ne of the rarest feats in baseball occurs when a player puts it all together during a season and wins the elusive Triple Crown. Only 14 players have ever accomplished this mastery, the last being Carl Yastrzemski of the Boston Red Sox during the 1967 season.

To win the Triple Crown a player must lead the league in home runs, runs batted in, and batting average. So not only does he have to hit for power, but he must also hit for average and have the luck to be at the plate with men in scoring position. Only two players have ever won the "Crown" twice. These winners were Ted Williams during the 1942 and 1947 seasons and Rogers Hornsby, playing for the St Louis Cardinals during 1922 and 1925.

With all the great players in the game, the Musials, the Ruths, the Dimaggios, only these few have captured the Triple Crown.

RIGHT: Ted Williams won the Triple Crown twice, in 1942 and 1947. He shares the record with Rogers Hornsby.

Hugh Duffy

TRIPLE CROWN WINNERS
AMERICAN LEAGUE

PLAYER	TEAM	YEAR	HOME RUNS	RBIs	AVE
Nap Lajoie	PHI	1901	14	125	.422
Ty Cobb	DET	1909	9	115	.377
Jimmy Foxx	PHI	1933	48	163	.356
Lou Gehrig	NY	1934	49	165	.363
Ted Williams	BOS	1942	36	137	.356
Ted Williams	BOS	1947	32	114	.343
Mickey Mantle	NY	1956	52	130	.353
Frank Robinson	BAL	1966	49	122	.316
Carl Yastrzemski	BOS	1967	44	121	.326

NATIONAL LEAGUE

PLAYER	TEAM	YEAR	HOME RUNS	RBIs	AVE
Paul Hines	PRO	1878	4	50	.358
Hugh Duffy	BOS	1894	18	145	.438
Heinie Zimmerman	CHI	1912	14	103	.372
Rogers Hornsby	STL	1922	42	152	.401
Rogers Hornsby	STL	1925	39	143	.403
Chuck Klein	PHI	1933	28	120	.368
Joe Medwick	STL	1937	31	154	.374

Joe Medwick

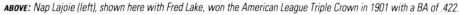

ABOVE: Nap Lajoie (left), shown here with Fred Lake, won the American League Triple Crown in 1901 with a BA of .422.

Most Career Runs Batted In

S ince the object for the batter is to cross home plate, the slugger who can break open a game with a run batted in (RBI) is a treasured part of the lineup. Some players, such as Hank Aaron, were able to drive in runners with alarming regularity. During his 23-year career, Hammerin' Hank drove in 100 or more runs 11 times, leading to a total of 2,297 RBIs.

Perhaps the most remarkable runs-batted-in record belongs to the Yankee's Lou Gehrig. Gehrig batted in over 100 men for 13 consecutive years! In 1931 Gehrig drove in a record of 184 men. Imagine the numbers Gehrig would have retired with if he hadn't been struck down with his career- and life-ending disease.

LEFT: William Bendix played the title role in the 1948 film The Babe Ruth Story.

MOST CAREER RUNS BATTED IN

PLAYER	RBIs
Henry Aaron	2297
Babe Ruth	2204
Lou Gehrig	1990
Ty Cobb	1960
Stan Musial	1951
Jimmy Foxx	1921
Willie Mays	1903
Mel Ott	1861
Carl Yastrzemski	1844
Ted Williams	1839
Al Simmons	1827
Frank Robinson	1812
Reggie Jackson	1702
Tony Perez	1652
Ernie Banks	1636
Goose Goslin	1609
Harmon Killebrew	1584
Al Kaline	1583
Rogers Hornsby	1578
Tris Speaker	1562
Willie McCovey	1555
Harry Heilmann	1551
Willie Stargell	1540
Joe DiMaggio	1537
Mike Schmidt	1505
Mickey Mantle	1509
Billy Williams	1476
Rusty Staub	1466
Eddie Mathews	1453
Yogi Berra	1430
Chuck Gehrenger	1427
Joe Cronin	1423
Jim Bottomley	1422
Joe Medwick	1383
Johnny Bench	1376
Orlando Cepeda	1365
Brooks Robinson	1357
Jim Rice	1351
Ted Simmons	1348
Johnny Mize	1337
Duke Snider	1333
Ron Santo	1331
Dave Winfield	1331
Al Oliver	1320
Pete Rose	1314
Jim Vernon	1311
Paul Waner	1309
Steve Garvey	1308
Ed Collins	1307
Roberto Clemente	1305
Enos Slaughter	1304
Del Ennis	1284
Bob Johnson	1283
Hank Greenberg	1276
Gil Hodges	1274
Pie Traynor	1273
Graig Nettles	1300
Zack Wheat	1265
Bobby Doerr	1247
Lee May	1244
Frankie Frisch	1242
George Foster	1239
Dave Kingman	1210
Bill Dickey	1209
Chuck Klein	1202

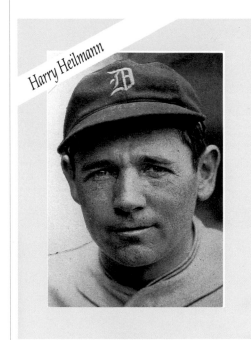

Harry Heilmann

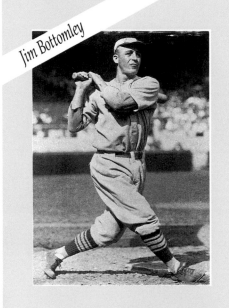

Jim Bottomley

Al Simmons

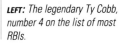

LEFT: The legendary Ty Cobb, number 4 on the list of most RBIs.

Most At-Bats, Doubleheaders

M any of us have experienced an extremely difficult, memorable day at the office. For a few major leaguers that particular memorable day seemed endless. For seven big leaguers, a certain doubleheader meant 14 at-bats. Some ballplayers have only 14 at-bats in a year!

Interestingly, these seven tired ballplayers accomplished their task during two very long doubleheaders. In the National League, Joe Christopher, Jim Hickman, Ed Kranepool, Roy McMillan and Frank Thomas, all from the New York Mets, were each credited with 14 at-bats during a May 31, 1964 doubleheader that lasted 32 innings.

The American League mark of 14 at-bats is shared by Robert Monday and Ramon Webster of the Kansas City Royals, who on June 17, 1967, played a 28-inning doubleheader.

MOST AT-BATS, DOUBLEHEADERS

NATIONAL LEAGUE

PLAYER	TEAM	INNINGS	AT-BATS	YEAR
Joe Christopher	New York	32	14	1964
Jim Hickman	New York	32	14	1964
Ed Kranepool	New York	32	14	1964
Roy McMillan	New York	32	14	1964
Frank Thomas	New York	32	14	1964
Rabbit Maranville	Pittsburgh	18	13	1922
Willie Herman	Chicago	18	13	1935

AMERICAN LEAGUE

PLAYER	TEAM	INNINGS	AT-BATS	YEAR
Bob Monday	Kansas City	28	14	1967
Ramon Webster	Kansas City	28	14	1967
Dave Philley	Chicago	18	13	1950

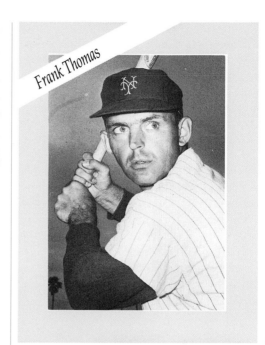

Frank Thomas

Jim Hickman

RIGHT: Joe Christopher.

Most Consecutive Years Leading League in Batting Average

A nybody who follows baseball statistics loves to catch the exploits of his favorite stars in the box scores. As the season heats up, it's exciting to watch the players compete for team as well as individual honors. For example, American League fans for the past few years have been treated to down-to-the-wire races for the league's batting champion. It seems as if Wade Boggs and Don Mattingly are always fighting for the title. Often the outcome isn't decided until the final game.

Certain players were supreme in their era. In the American League, Ty Cobb of the Detroit Tigers led through 1915. Rogers Hornsby holds the National League record, capturing the title for six straight years from 1920 through 1925.

BELOW: Ty Cobb led the American League in batting average from 1907 to 1915.

MOST CONSECUTIVE YEARS LEADING IN BATTING AVERAGE

PLAYER	YEARS	TEAM	DATES
Ty Cobb	9	Detroit AL	1907–1915
Rogers Hornsby	6	St. Louis NL	1920–1925

BELOW: Rogers Hornsby (center) led the National League in batting average from 1920 to 1925. He is shown here with Hack Wilson (left) and Kiki Cuyler (right).

The .400 Club

A s 30 wins are to a pitcher, hitting .400 is the magical mark for a batter. The mark has been so rarely achieved that the last player to reach the goaal was Ted Williams, playing for the 1941 Boston Red Sox.

The chances of another batter hitting .400 for a season have become even more difficult because of night games, relief pitchers, and the longer season. Active players who have a chance someday to join the exclusive .400 club include such contact hitters as George Brett, Don Mattingly, and of course Wade Boggs. Brett, in fact, came the closest when in 1980 he hit .390 after flirting with the magic number for most of the season.

THE .400 CLUB
AMERICAN LEAGUE

PLAYER	TEAM	YEAR	AVERAGE
Nap Lajoie	Philadelphia	1901	.422
Ty Cobb	Detroit	1911	.420
George Sisler	St. Louis	1922	.420
Ty Cobb	Detroit	1912	.410
Joe Jackson	Cleveland	1911	.408
George Sisler	St. Louis	1920	.407
Ted Williams	Boston	1941	.406
Harry Heilman	Detroit	1923	.403
Ty Cobb	Detroit	1922	.401

NATIONAL LEAGUE

PLAYER	TEAM	YEAR	AVERAGE
Hugh Duffy	Boston	1894	.438
Willie Keeler	Baltimore	1897	.432
Rogers Hornsby	St. Louis	1924	.424
Jesse Burkett	Cleveland	1895	.423
Jesse Burkett	Cleveland	1896	.410
Ed Delahanty	Philadelphia	1899	.408
Fred Clarke	Louisville	1897	.406
Sam Thompson	Philadelphia	1894	.404
Rogers Hornsby	St. Louis	1925	.403
Jesse Burkett	St. Louis	1899	.402
Rogers Hornsby	St. Louis	1922	.401
Bill Terry	New York	1930	.401
Ed Delahanty	Philadelphia	1894	.400

Ted Williams

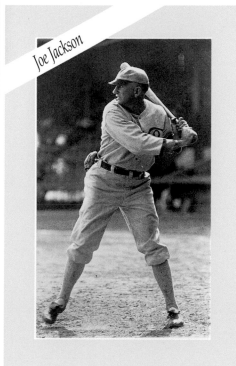

Joe Jackson

ABOVE: *The American League branch of the exclusive .400 club is lead by Nap Lajoie.*

Highest Career Batting Average

Since the ultimate object of any batter is getting a hit, those with the most success get the highest batting averages. It's one thing to have a high average for a season or two, but to end your career with a respectable batting average is quite a feat. To make a list of the highest career averages, it's only fair to limit it to those who played either ten years or had at least 1,000 hits. After all, the history of the game has many players who played only a few years before injuries or other circumstances forced their early retirement.

The leader in lifetime batting average is Ty Cobb of the Detroit Tigers. Cobb batted .367 during his 24 years as a major leaguer. Surprisingly, Babe Ruth, known more for his home-run hitting than his high batting average, makes the list. Ruth batted .342 during his 22-year career.

Of the active players, Boston's Wade Boggs, who won batting titles in 1983, 1985, and 1986, and Don Mattingly, winner in 1984, have the best chance of cracking the all-time list when their playing days are over.

HIGHEST CAREER BATTING AVERAGE

PLAYER	YEARS	HITS	AVERAGE
Ty Cobb	24	4191	.367
Rogers Hornsby	23	2930	.358
Joe Jackson	13	1772	.356
Pete Browning	13	1719	.354
David Orr	8	1163	.352
Dennis Brouthers	19	2349	.349
Frank O'Doul	11	1140	.349
Ed Delahanty	16	2593	.346
Tris Speaker	22	3515	.345
Willie Keeler	19	2955	.345
Ted Williams	19	2654	.344
Billy Hamilton	14	2157	.344
Jake Stenzel	9	1028	.344
Babe Ruth	22	2873	.342
Jesse Burkett	16	2872	.342
Harry Heilmann	17	2660	.342
Bill Terry	14	2193	.341
George Sisler	15	2812	.340
Lou Gehrig	17	2721	.340
Jim O'Neill	10	1428	.340
Nap Lajoie	21	3252	.339
Cap Anson	22	3081	.339
Sam Thompson	15	2016	.336
Riggs Stephenson	14	1515	.336
William Lange	7	1072	.336
Al Simmons	20	2927	.334
John McGraw	16	1307	.334
Mike Donlin	12	1287	.334
Ed Collins	25	3309	.333
Paul Waner	20	3152	.333
Stan Musial	22	3630	.331
Dennis Lyons	13	1404	.331
Heinie Manush	17	2524	.330
Hugh Duffy	17	2307	.330
Honus Wagner	21	3430	.329
Rod Carew	19	3053	.328
Robert Fothergill	12	1064	.325
Jimmy Foxx	20	2646	.325
Roger Connor	18	2535	.325
Joe DiMaggio	13	2214	.325
Edd Roush	16	2158	.325
Earle Combs	12	1866	.325
Joe Medwick	17	2471	.324
Floyd Herman	13	1818	.324
Ed Rice	20	2987	.322
Ross Youngs	10	1491	.322
George VanHaltren	17	2573	.321
Kiki Cuyler	18	2299	.321
Joe Kelley	17	2245	.321
Harry Stovey	14	1925	.321
Charlie Gehringer	19	2839	.320
Pie Traynor	17	2416	.320
Chuck Klein	17	2076	.320
Mickey Cochrane	13	1652	.320
Jim Holliday	10	1152	.320
Ken Williams	14	1552	.319
Arky Vaughan	14	2103	.318
Earl Averill	13	2019	.318
Roberto Clemente	18	3000	.317
Zack Wheat	19	2884	.317
Mike Tiernan	13	1875	.317
Chick Hafey	13	1466	.317
Joe Harris	10	963	.317
Lloyd Waner	18	2459	.316
Frank Frisch	19	2880	.316
Leon Goslin	18	2735	.316
Henry Larkin	10	1493	.316
Lew Fonseca	12	1075	.316
Fred Clarke	21	2703	.315
Elmer Flick	13	1767	.315
John Tobin	11	1579	.315
Jimmy Ryan	18	2577	.314
Jim O'Rourke	19	2314	.314
Cecil Travis	12	1544	.314
Hugh Jennings	18	1520	.314
Elmer Smith	14	1473	.314
Bibb Falk	12	1463	.314
George Brett	14	2095	.314
Bill Dickey	17	1969	.313
Michael Kelly	16	1853	.313
Jack Fournier	15	1631	.313
Hank Greenberg	13	1628	.313
Joe Sewell	14	2226	.312
Johnny Mize	15	2011	.312
Ed Miller	16	1937	.312
Clarence Childs	13	1757	.312
Barney McCosky	11	1301	.312
Dale Mitchell	11	1244	.312
Ginger Beaumont	12	1754	.311
Fred Lindstrom	13	1747	.311
Bill Jacobson	11	1714	.311
Bill Ewing	18	1663	.311
Jackie Robinson	10	1518	.311
Rip Radcliff	10	1267	.311
Taft Wright	9	1115	.311
Luke Appling	20	2749	.310
Jim Bottomley	16	2313	.310
Ed McKean	13	2139	.310
Bobby Veach	14	2064	.310
Irish Meusel	11	1521	.310
Tom Burns	11	1451	.310

LEFT: Dave Parker.

Joe Jackson

Manny Mota	20	1149	.304
Jake Daubert	15	2326	.303
Charles Myer	17	2131	.303
Harvey Kuenn	15	2092	.303
Charles Jameson	18	1990	.303
George Harper	11	1030	.303
Earl Smith	12	686	.303
John Stivetts	11	592	.303
Al Oliver	18	2743	.303
Pete Rose	24	4256	.303
Jim Rice	13	2163	.303
Ben Chapman	15	1958	.302
Hal Trosky	11	1561	.302
George F. Grantham	13	1508	.302
Tom Holmes	11	1507	.302
Carl Reynolds	13	1357	.302
Piano Legs Hickman	12	1199	.302
Homer Summa	10	905	.302

Sam Hale	10	880	.302
Bob Caruthers	10	758	.302
John Doyle	17	1814	.302
Willie Mays	22	3283	.302
Keith Hernandez	13	1840	.302
Joe Cronin	20	2285	.301
Stan Hack	16	2193	.301
Ray Bressler	19	1170	.301
John Mostil	10	1054	.301
Ray Blades	10	726	.301
Dave Parker	14	2024	.301
Enos Slaughter	19	2383	.300
Bill Goodman	16	1691	.300
Wally Berger	11	1550	.300
Ethan Allen	13	1325	.300
Earl Sheely	9	1340	.300
Ken Griffey	14	1839	.300
Cecil Cooper	16	2130	.300

The leader in lifetime batting average is Ty Cobb, who ended his 24-year career with an astounding average of .367!

Jonathan Stone	11	1391	.310
Eugene Hargrave	12	786	.310
Gordon Phelps	11	657	.310
Sam Crawford	19	2964	.309
Jake Beckley	20	2930	.309
Bob Meusel	11	1693	.309
Richie Ashburn	15	2574	.308
John McInnis	19	2406	.308
Steve Brodie	12	1749	.308
George Gore	14	1653	.308
Virgil Davis	16	1312	.308
Harvey Hendrick	11	896	.308
Eugene DeMontreville	11	1106	.308
George Burns	16	2018	.307
Frank Baker	13	1838	.307
Michael Griffin	12	1830	.307
Joseph Vosmik	13	1682	.307
Chick Stahl	10	1552	.307
Lew Wilson	12	1461	.307
Johnny Pesky	10	1455	.307
Fred Leach	10	1147	.307
John Moore	10	926	.307
Henry Bonura	8	1099	.307
Matty Alou	15	1777	.307
Bill Madlock	14	1906	.307
Fred Walker	18	2064	.306
George Kell	15	2054	.306
Ernie Lombardi	17	1792	.306
James White	15	1612	.306
Charley Jones	11	1062	.306
Ralph Garr	13	1562	.306
Henry Aaron	23	3771	.305
Tim Raines	8	1028	.305
Mel Ott	22	2876	.304
Bill Herman	15	2345	.304
Pat Donovan	17	2254	.304
Paul Hines	16	1884	.304
Ben Seymour	16	1720	.304
Harding Richardson	14	1705	.304
Curtis Walker	12	1475	.304
Sam Leslie	10	749	.304
Tony Oliva	15	1917	.304

Most Career Pinch Hits

B aseball has few specialty positions. Besides the relief pitcher, the next most important part-time role is that of the pinch hitter. In the history of baseball, some players have distinguished themselves by being able to come off the bench and wield the bat to punch out a hit. It's not an easy task. While the other players are loosened up, the pinch hitter has been idle, watching the game from the dugout or even the locker room.

Some pinch hitters, like Jerry Lynch of the Cincinnati Reds, were specialists in crushing home runs. During his career Lynch smoked 18 pinch-hit homers. Other pinch hitters, like Smokey Burgess of the White Sox and Rusty Staub of the Mets, were able to extend their playing days after remarkable years as everyday players by their amazing ability to pinch hit.

Manny Mota of the Los Angeles Dodgers displayed his pinch-hitting skills by coming through with three hits in seven attempts during the Dodgers' pennant race in 1980.

BELOW: *Manny Mota holds the record for most career pinch hits with 150.*

José Morales

Rusty Staub

MOST CAREER PINCH HITS

PLAYER	PINCH HITS
Manny Mota	150
Smokey Burgess	145
José Morales	123
Jerry Lynch	116
Red Lucas	114
Terry Crowley	108
Gates Brown	107
Mike Lum	103
Steve Braun	102
Vic Davalillo	95
Larry Bittner	95
Dave Philley	93
Ed Kranepool	90
Elmer Valo	90
Jay Johnstone	90
Rusty Staub	89
Greg Gross	88
Jesus Alou	82
Tim McCarver	82
Dalton Jones	81
Tito Francona	81
Tom Hutton	79
Kurt Bevacqua	77
Enos Slaughter	77
Bob Fothergill	76
George Crowe	76
Jerry Turner	73
Ed Kirkpatrick	71
Jimmy Stewart	71
Bob Skinner	69
Mike Jorgensen	69
Champ Summers	68
Ron Fairly	68
Merv Rettenmund	66
Bob Johnson	66
Willie McCovey	66
Ernie Lombardi	66
Ken Boswell	66
Gene Woodling	65
Oscar Gamble	64
Tommy Davis	63
Tony Taylor	63
Julio Becquer	63
Jim King	63
Peanuts Lowrey	62
Bob Bailey	62
Vic Wertz	62
Bob Hale	62
Mike Vail	61
Cliff Johnson	60
Ty Cline	60
Ron Northey	59
Sam Leslie	59
Russ Nixon	59
Duke Snider	59
Clarence Gaston	59
Gene Clines	59
Jim Dwyer	59
Red Ruffing	58
Denny Walling	57
Jerry Hairston	57
Ham Hyatt	57
Wes Covington	57
Lee Maye	57
Red Schoendienst	56
José Pagan	56
Fred Whitfield	56
Lee Lacy	56
Charlie Maxwell	56
Walker Cooper	56
Billy Sullivan	55
Earl Torgeson	55
Bob Cerv	55
Len Gabrielson	55
John Lowenstein	55
Willie Stargell	55
Dusty Rhodes	55
Phil Gagliano	55
Frenchy Bordagaray	54
Debs Garms	54
Willie Smith	54
Del Unser	54
Johnny Mize	53
Ted Kluszewski	53
Lenny Green	53
Dane Iorg	52
Dom Dallessandro	52
Walt Williams	52
Irv Noren	52
Jim Wohlford	52
Larry Stahl	52
Harvey Hendrick	51
Glenn Adams	51
Pat Kelly	51
Dick Williams	51
John Milner	51
José Cardenal	50

.400 Seasons by Pinch Hitters

Modern teams always keep a few available batters on the bench. When the game is on the line and a base hit is desperately needed, the manager selects his pinch hitter.

A pinch hitter, after riding the bench for a good part of the game, must be able to turn on the hitting switch. Some are more successful than others. Of those pinch hitters with at least 35 at-bats in a season, Ed Kranepool leads the pack. For the 1974 New York Mets, Kranepool went 17 for 35 as a pinch hitter, yielding a batting average of .486.

The San Francisco Giants' Candy Maldonado pinch hit in 1986 at a .425 clip, good enough to earn him a starting role the following season.

A quality pinch hitter can prolong his career by possessing the ability to get those emergency hits. Such modern-day players as Rusty Staub, Lee Mazzili, and Davey Lopes all extended their playing days with the pinch hit.

.400 SEASONS BY PINCH HITTERS

PLAYER	TEAM	YEAR	HITS	AT-BATS	AVE
Ed Kranepool	New York Mets	1974	17	35	.486
Gates Brown	Detroit Tigers	1968	18	39	.472
Frenchy Bordagaray	St. Louis Cards	1938	20	43	.465
Rick Miller	Boston Red Sox	1983	16	35	.457
José Pagan	Pittsburgh Pirates	1969	19	42	.452
Joe Cronin	Boston Red Sox	1942	18	42	.429
Don Dillard	Cleveland Indians	1961	15	35	.429
Candy Maldonado	San Francisco Giants	1986	17	40	.425
Merritt Ranew	Chicago Cubs	1963	17	41	.415
Carl Taylor	Pittsburgh Pirates	1969	17	41	.415
Dave Philley	Philadelphia Phils	1958	18	44	.409
Frankie Baumholtz	Chicago Cubs	1955	15	37	.405
Jerry Lynch	Cincinnati Reds	1961	19	47	.404
Jerry Turner	San Diego Padres	1978	20	50	.400
Chet Laabs	St. Louis Browns	1940	14	35	.400

Gates Brown

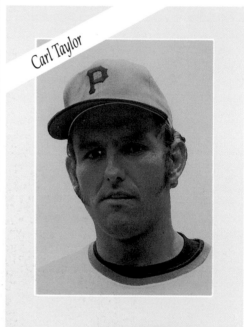

Carl Taylor

Candy Maldonado

Rick Miller

LEFT: Doc Dillard.

Consecutive-Game Hitting Streak

Perhaps the hardest records to break are those that require longevity and endurance. Besides Lou Gehrig's consecutive game mark, the other seemingly impossible achievement is Joe DiMaggio's 56-game hitting streak. The latest pretender to the throne, the legendary Pete Rose, finally caved in to the media pressure in 1978 and finished with 44 games, tying him with Willie Keeler's mark.

DiMaggio's awesome hitting display lasted for over two months. Beginning on May 15, 1941, and lasting until July 17, DiMaggio banged out hits in a record 56 consecutive games. The streak ended when Al Smith an Jim Bagby of the Cleveland Indians finally shut down Joltin' Joe. Then the next day, DiMaggio went on a mini-streak, getting hits in an additional 16 games. One of the purest hitters in the game, DiMaggio's record will be close to impossible to break. In 1987 Benito Santiago of San Diego hit in 34 straight games – a record for a rookie and also a record for a major-league catcher.

Player	Team	Year	Games
John Stone	DET	1930	27
Heinie Manush	WAS	1930	27
Al Simmons	PHI	1931	27
Luke Appling	CHI	1936	27
Gee Walker	DET	1936	27
Bruce Campbell	DET	1941	27
Bob Dillinger	STL	1948	27
Dom DiMaggio	BOS	1951	27
Dale Mitchell	CLE	1953	27
Ron LeFlore	DET	1978	27
Buck Freeman	BOS	1902	26
Harry Bay	CLE	1902	26
Hobe Ferris	STL	1908	26
Babe Ruth	NY	1921	26
Heinie Manush	WAS	1933	26
Bob Johnson	PHI	1934	26
Guy Curtright	CHI	1943	26
Johnny Pesky	BOS	1947	26
Ty Cobb	DET	1906	25
Bucky Harris	WAS	1925	25
Goose Goslin	WAS	1928	25
Catfish Metkovich	BOS	1944	25
Jimmy Foxx	PHI	1929	24
Cecil Travis	WAS	1941	24
Chico Carrasquel	CHI	1950	24
Ferris Fain	PHI	1952	24
Lenny Green	MIN	1961	24
Dave May	MIL	1973	24
Mickey Rivers	TEX	1980	24

NATIONAL LEAGUE

PLAYER	TEAM	YEAR	GAMES
Willie Keeler	BAL	1897	44
Pete Rose	CIN	1978	44
Bill Dahlen	CHI	1894	42
Tommy Holmes	BOS	1945	37
Billy Hamilton	BOS	1896	36
Fred Clarke	LOU	1895	35
Benito Santiago	SD	1987	34
George Davis	NY	1893	33
Rogers Hornsby	STL	1922	33
Ed Delahanty	PHI	1899	31
Willie Davis	LA	1969	31
Rico Carty	ATL	1970	31
Elmer Smith	CIN	1898	30
Stan Musial	STL	1950	30
Zack Wheat	BKN	1916	29
Harry Walker	STL	1943	29
Ken Boyer	STL	1959	29
Rowland Office	ATL	1976	29
Lloyd Waner	PIT	1932	28
Joe Medwick	STL	1935	28
Red Schoendienst	STL	1954	28
Ron Santo	CHI	1966	28
Piano Legs Hickman	NY	1900	27
Edd Roush	CIN	1920	27
Edd Roush	CIN	1924	27
Hack Wilson	CHI	1929	27

CONSECUTIVE-GAME HITTING STREAK
AMERICAN LEAGUE

PLAYER	TEAM	YEAR	GAMES
Joe DiMaggio	NY	1941	56
George Sisler	STL	1922	41
Ty Cobb	DET	1911	40
Paul Molitor	MIL	1987	39
Ty Cobb	DET	1917	35
George Sisler	STL	1925	34
John Stone	DET	1930	34
George McQuinn	STL	1938	34
Dom DiMaggio	BOS	1949	34
Heinie Manush	WAS	1934	33
Sam Rice	WAS	1924	31
Ken Landreaux	MIN	1980	31
Tris Speaker	BOS	1912	30
Goose Goslin	DET	1934	30
Ron LeFlore	DET	1976	30
George Brett	KC	1980	30
Bill Bradley	CLE	1902	29
Roger Peckinpaugh	NY	1919	29
Bill Lamar	PHI	1925	29
Dale Alexander	DET	1930	29
Earle Combs	NY	1931	29
Pete Fox	DET	1935	29
Mel Almada	STL	1938	29
Joe Gordon	NY	1942	29
Nap Lajoie	PHI	1901	28
Joe Jackson	CLE	1911	28
Ken Williams	STL	1922	28
Bing Miller	PHI	1929	28
Sam Rice	WAS	1930	28
Heinie Manush	WAS	1932	28
Doc Cramer	PHI	1932	28
Hal Trosky	CLE	1936	28
Socks Seybold	PHI	1901	27
Hal Chase	NY	1907	27
Sam Rice	WAS	1925	27

Joe Medwick	BKN	1942	27
Duke Snider	BKN	1953	27
Vada Pinson	CIN	1965	27
Glenn Beckert	CHI	1968	27
Willie Keeler	BAL	1896	26
George Decker	CHI	1896	26
Bill Sweeney	BOS	1911	26
Zack Wheat	BKN	1918	26
Goldie Rapp	PHI	1921	26
Pie Traynor	PIT	1923	26
Chuck Klein	PHI	1930	26
Chuck Klein	PHI	1930	26
Gabby Hartnett	CHI	1937	26
Danny O'Connell	PIT	1953	26
Lou Brock	STL	1971	26
Glenn Beckert	CHI	1973	26
Jack Clark	SF	1978	26
Clyde Barnhart	PIT	1925	25
Rube Bressler	CIN	1927	25
Hughie Critz	CIN	1927	25
Harvey Hendrick	BKN	1929	25
Charlie Grimm	CHI	1933	25
Fred Lindstrom	PIT	1933	25
Buzz Boyle	BKN	1934	25
Hank Aaron	MIL	1956	25
Hank Aaron	MIL	1962	25
Pete Rose	CIN	1967	25
Willie Davis	LA	1971	25

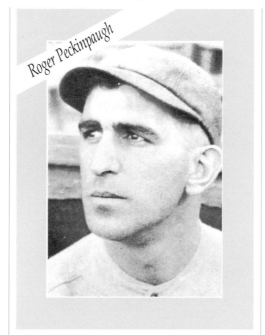

Roger Peckinpaugh

Rowland Office

Dale Alexander

RIGHT: *Joe DiMaggio's brother Dom hit in 27 straight games in 1951.*

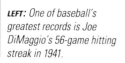

LEFT: *One of baseball's greatest records is Joe DiMaggio's 56-game hitting streak in 1941.*

Most Years Leading League in Hits

A ny time a hitting record is involved, a statistics expert will look for the names of Ty Cobb and Pete Rose. So if we want the American and National League players who have led the league in hits the most times, just pencil in the dynamic duo.

Ty Cobb lead all American League players in hits eight times, although he had to settle for a tie with Detroit's Bob Veach in 1919. Pete Rose bested all National Leaguers seven times, although he was tied with Felipe Alou in 1968 and Billy Williams in 1970.

Another leader of the hit parade was Tony Oliva of the Minnesota Twins. Oliva out-hit his American League contemporaries five times.

Today's big hitters include George Brett, Don Mattingly, Wade Boggs, and Tony Gwynn of the San Diego Padres.

MOST YEARS LEADING IN HITS

PLAYER	YEARS	TEAM	YEARS
Ty Cobb	8	Detroit AL	1907
			1908
			1909
			1911
			1912
			1915
			1917
			1919 (tied)
Pete Rose	7	Cincinnati 7	1965
			1968 (tied)
			1970 (tied)
			1972
			1973
			1976
		Philadelphia NL	1981

BELOW: Ty Cobb led the American League in hits for seven seasons, and tied for the lead in one.

LEFT: Pete Rose tied for the National League hits lead twice and led five times.

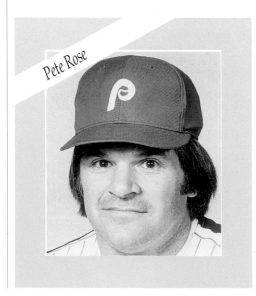

Pete Rose

Most Consecutive Years Leading League in Hits

T he games' greatest hitters are capable of putting some remarkable numbers on the board. By keeping their batting eyes well-focused, those masters of disaster at the plate rise to the top in yearly offensive statistics. Although no player has ever led his league in most hits more than eight times, seven exceptional batters had the most hits for three consecutive years.

In the National League, Clarence Beaumont, Rogers Hornsby, Frank McCormick, and Stan Musial each put together three consecutive years in leading the league in hits. Musial made the list even though Thomas Holmes of the Boston Braves led the league in 1945. Since Musial served in World War II during the 1945 season, the league's statistics allowed that year to be omitted in compiling consecutive year records. After the war, Musial picked up his bat and resumed his hitting exhibition, banging out 228 hits to lead the league.

The American League three-timers are Ty Cobb, John Pesky, and Tony Oliva. Pesky's feat is considerable since he led the league in 1942, spent three years in the armed forces, and then returned, getting the most hits in 1946 and 1947!

Frank McCormick

Johnny Pesky

ABOVE: *Ty Cobb (right) compares notes with Honus Wagner (center).*

MOST CONSECUTIVE YEARS LEADING IN HITS

PLAYER	YEARS	TEAM	YEARS
Clarence Beaumont	3	Pittsburgh NL	1902
			1903
			1904
Ty Cobb	3	Detroit AL	1907
			1908
			1909
Rogers Hornsby	3	St. Louis NL	1920
			1921
			1922
Frank McCormick	3	Cincinnati NL	1938
			1939
			1940 (tied)
Stan Musial	3	St. Louis NL	1943
			1944
			1946 (military service 1945)
Johnny Pesky	3	Boston AL	1942
			1946
			1947 (military service 1943, 1944, 1945)
Tony Oliva	3	Minnesota	1964
			1965
			1966

Most Career At-Bats

One way to measure a player's longevity is by compiling the number of career at-bats. Some players extend their careers by being used as pinch-hitters or simply reducing their playing time. Others like Carl Yastrzemski and Stan Musial maintained active careers until retirement.

The leader of the at-bat pack is Pete Rose, who came to the plate 14,053 times in his career. Just the players with 10,000 or more at-bats give us many of the game's greats. Hank Aaron, Ty Cobb, Willie Mays, Brooks Robinson, and Lou Brock are some members of the 10,000 plus club. To make the list, a player must have had an extended career. A modern player, who averages 600 at-bats per year, would have to play for almost 17 years to reach the magic 10,000 plateau.

Today's modern coaching and training methods make it plausible to believe that others are destined for the list. Don Mattingly, Cal Ripken, and Wade Boggs are the type of players fully capable of amassing large numbers of at-bats.

RIGHT: *Honus Wagner*

Ernie Banks

RIGHT: *Vada Pinson*

Player	At-Bats
Frank Robinson	10006
Ed Collins	9946
Reggie Jackson	9864
Tony Perez	9778
Rusty Staub	9720
Vada Pinson	9645
Nap Lajoie	9589
Sam Crawford	9579
Jake Beckley	9476
Paul Waner	9459
Mel Ott	9456
Roberto Clemente	9454
Ernie Banks	9421
Max Carey	9363
Billy Williams	9350
Rod Carew	9315
Joe Morgan	9277
Ed Rice	9269
Nellie Fox	9232
Bill Davis	9174
Roger Cramer	9140
Frank Frisch	9112
Zack Wheat	9106
Cap Anson	9084
Lafayette Cross	9065
Al Oliver	9049
George Davis	9027
Bill Dahlen	9019

MOST CAREER AT-BATS

PLAYER	AT-BATS
Pete Rose	14053
Henry Aaron	12364
Carl Yastrzemski	11988
Ty Cobb	11429
Stan Musial	10972
Willie Mays	10881
Brooks Robinson	10654
Honus Wagner	10427
Lou Brock	10332
Luis Aparicio	10230
Tris Speaker	10196
Al Kaline	10116
Rabbit Maranville	10078

Max Carey

Most Hits in a Season

S ingles, doubles, triples, or home runs – in the category of hits, they all count. Every time a player swings the bat, he's trying to get a hit. Since the better players get about 500 at-bats a season, and a .300 average is considered good, they can expect anywhere from 150 to 170 hits. However, the game's best players have been able to put extraordinary numbers on the boards.

George Sisler, of the old St. Louis Browns, holds the American League record for most hits in a season with 257 in 1920. In the past ten years, Rod Carew finished with 239 hits in 1977; Don Mattingly banged out 238.

Over in the National League, Philadelphia's Frank O'Doul in 1929 and New York Giant Bill Terry in 1930 share the honors with 254. The players that have come close to that mark are Joe Torre with 230 in 1971 and Mattie Alou with 231 in 1969. Of course, never one to be left off a statistics list, Pete Rose slammed 230 hits for the 1973 Cincinnati Reds.

LEFT: The record for most hits in a season is 257, set by George Sisler in 1920.

MOST HITS IN A SEASON

PLAYER	HITS	GAMES	TEAM	YEAR
George Sisler	257	154	St. Louis AL	1920
Frank O'Doul	254	154	Philadelphia NL	1929
Bill Terry	254	154	New York NL	1930

RIGHT: Frank O'Doul

Bill Terry

Most Games with One or More Hits in a Season

Considering that each team only plays 162 games, it seems that this category is very limited. However, if like so many other fans, you've ever pored over a box score, you appreciate the fact that some of the greatest in the game were able to crack the hit column so many times.

The American League record is held by a player many people consider the next threat to bat .400. Playing for the same team as the last .400 hitter, Ted Williams, Boston's Wade Boggs is a machine at the plate. His smooth swing sliced through the air in 1985 and made enough contact to bang out at least one hit in 135 games. Playing in 161 games that year, Boggs got one hit in more than 80 per cent of those efforts.

Rogers Hornsby and Chuck Klein share the National League record of 135. Since Hornsby played in 154 games and Klein 156, that means these incredible batsmen got at least one hit in over 87 per cent of the games.

MOST GAMES WITH ONE OR MORE HITS IN A SEASON

PLAYER	HITS	GAMES	TEAM	YEAR
Rogers Hornsby	135	154	St. Louis NL	1922
Chuck Klein	135	156	Philadelphia NL	1930
Wade Boggs	135	161	Boston AL	1985

LEFT: Slugger Wade Boggs hit safely at least once in 135 games in 1985.

ABOVE: Chuck Klein got one or more hits 135 times in the 1930 season.

The 3,000 Hit Club

I f you look at a list of those players with the greatest number of hits, you'll see that only 16 have cracked 3,000 or more. Of course, most of the leaders are well-known players such as Pete Rose and Ty Cobb. But you have to move well down the list to find some other great ballplayers, like Babe Ruth and Lou Gehrig.

Pete Rose, now the manager of the Cincinnati Reds, is the all-time leader of the pack with 4,256 hits. Statistic buffs knew that Rose had a chance to eclipse Ty Cobb's record when Rose, during his 16th season, smacked hit 3,000, a mark reached by Cobb in his 17th season. After hitting number 3,000, Rose methodically stalked the great legend, banging out base hits. Never a power hitter, Rose finished with 3,215 singles. Rose, known as Charlie Hustle for his aggressive play, was often compared to Cobb. So it's not surprising to find that Cobb, the second most productive player of the game, finished his career with 3,052 singles, second only to Rose.

RIGHT: *Peter Rose*

THE 3,000 HIT CLUB	
PLAYER	HITS
Pete Rose	4256
Ty Cobb	4191
Henry Aaron	3771
Stan Musial	3630
Tris Speaker	3515
Honus Wagner	3430
Carl Yastrzemski	3419
Eddie Collins	3309
Willie Mays	3283
Nap Lajoie	3252
Paul Waner	3152
Cap Anson	3081
Rod Carew	3053
Lou Brock	3023
Al Kaline	3007
Roberto Clemente	3000

RIGHT: *Lou Brock*

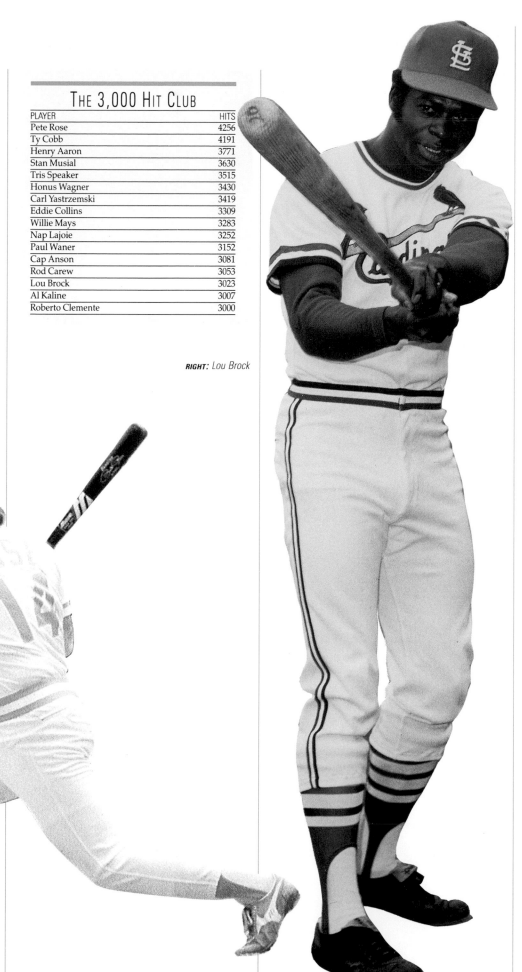

200 Hits in a Season

With all the available statistics surrounding the game of baseball, for batters the mark of 200 hits in a season is a noted milestone. Like a pitcher's 20 wins in a year, 200 hits seem to indicate that the player had a special season. It should come as no surprise that Pete Rose is on top of the list, having had ten seasons of 200 hits.

Rose, always kept abreast of where he stood in the record books, took pride in finishing his career with one more 200-hit season than the legendary Ty Cobb. Finishing behind Cobb and Rose, with eight seasons, Lou Gehrig and 'Wee Willie Keeler established themselves as masters with the bat.

Of today's current crop of batters, you need only to check out the yearly batting-average leader to see that Wade Boggs, Don Mattingly, and San Diego's Tony Gwynn are piling up the 200-hit seasons.

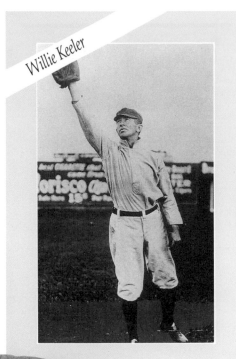

Willie Keeler

ABOVE: Jim Rice

200 HITS IN A SEASON

PLAYER	YEARS
Pete Rose	10
Ty Cobb	9
Lou Gehrig	8
Willie Keeler	8
Paul Waner	8
Charlie Gehringer	7
Rogers Hornsby	7
Jesse Burkett	6
Stan Musial	6
Ed Rice	6
Al Simmons	6
George Sisler	6
Bill Terry	6
Steve Garvey	6
Chuck Klein	5
Nap Lajoie	5
Wade Boggs	5
Vada Pinson	4
Harry Heilmann	4
Joe Jackson	4
Heinie Manush	4
Joe Medwick	4
Tris Speaker	4
John Tobin	4
Lloyd Waner	4
Roberto Clemente	4
Lou Brock	4
Rod Carew	4
Jim Rice	4

LEFT: Pete Rose got 200 hits in a season ten times, making him first on the list.

Most Hits, First Game in Majors

I magine how nervous a player must get, sitting in the dugout prior to his first major-league game. With family and friends in the stands, for many it's the biggest day of their lives. The public-address announcer tells the crowd the rookie's name and seconds later another major-league career commences. For many, facing major-league pitching for the first time is a humiliating experience. But for those fortunate enough to rise to the occasion, it's a day for the record books.

The record for most hits by a rookie in his first game is shared by ten players. These exceptional ten got their hits in a regulation nine-inning game. (Cecil Travis of the 1933 Washington Senators stroked five singles in a 12-inning game.) For some, like Willie McCovey, the hot opening led to a distinguished career. But most of these rookies drifted back to mediocrity. However, Casey Stengel later made his mark as one of the game's greatest managers, and Kirby Puckett, an all-star outfielder for the Minnesota Twins, has become one of the best young players in the American League.

MOST HITS, FIRST GAME IN MAJORS
AMERICAN LEAGUE

PLAYER	HITS	TEAM	YEAR
Ray Jansen	4	St. Louis	1910
Charlie Shires	4	Chicago	1928
Russ Van Atta	4	New York	1933
Forrest Jacobs	4	Philadelphia	1954
Ted Cox	4	Boston	1977
Kirby Puckett	4	Minnesota	1984

NATIONAL LEAGUE

PLAYER	HITS	TEAM	YEAR
Casey Stengel	4	Brooklyn	1917
Ed Freed	4	Philadelphia	1942
Willie McCovey	4	San Francisco	1959
Mack Jones	4	Milwaukee	1961

Kirby Puckett

LEFT: *Casey Stengel, better known as a manager than as a player, is the first of four National League players to get four hits in his first game in the majors.*

200 or More Hits, Rookie Season

S ince reaching the magic yearly 200-hit figure is the goal of every ballplayer, imagine what an accomplishment it must be for a rookie. In the history of the game, only 12 rookies have successfully reached that plateau. To get 200 hits, a rookie needs more than talent. He must be good enough to crack the starting lineup and then be hot enough with the bat to stay there. Every year a new crop of talented, highly touted rookies makes the majors. Yet by the end of the season, only a select few have left any lasting impressions.

Glory is so fleeting, in fact, that some of the rookies on this list faded quickly. A few, however, just proved that their rookie year was the start of something big. Such superstars as Richie Allen, Lloyd Waner, Joe DiMaggio, John Pesky, Harvey Kuenn, and Tony Oliva all belted out at least 200 hits during their rookie year. Tony Oliva was so good that not only did he lead the American League with 217 hits in 1964, but he won the batting crown, hitting .323. Oliva then went on to lead the league in hits four more times and win two more batting titles in 1965 and 1971.

200 OR MORE HITS, ROOKIE SEASON
NATIONAL LEAGUE

PLAYER	HITS	GAMES	TEAM	YEAR
Lloyd Waner	223	150	Pittsburgh	1927
Jim Williams	219	153	Pittsburgh	1899
Johnny Frederick	206	148	Brooklyn	1929
Richie Allen	201	162	Philadelphia	1964

AMERICAN LEAGUE

PLAYER	HITS	GAMES	TEAM	YEAR
Tony Oliva	217	161	Minnesota	1964
Dale Alexander	215	155	Detroit	1929
Kevin Seitzer	209	161	Kansas City	1987
Harvey Kuenn	209	155	Detroit	1953
Joe DiMaggio	206	138	New York	1936
Hal Trosky	206	154	Cleveland	1934
Johnny Pesky	205	147	Boston	1942
Roy Johnson	201	148	Detroit	1929
Dick Wakefield	200	155	Detroit	1943

BELOW: Richie Allen

Dick Wakefield

RIGHT: Johnny Pesky

Most Career Singles

While fans of baseball holler for a batter to belt the ball out of the park, some of the game's greatest players were better suited to hitting singles. The all-time leader in the singles standing is Pete Rose with 3,215, just 63 ahead of Ty Cobb's 3,052. Then the list drops down to the two thousands, where such notables as Eddie Collins, Wee Willie Keeler, and Rod Carew are camped out.

Checking the list, a few of the games long-ball hitters have made the singles list. The all-time home-run leader, Hank Aaron, finished his career with 2,294 single-baggers. Carl Yastrzemski banged out 2,262 singles. Most of the players on the list were known for their finesse with the bat. From Roberto Clemente to Nellie Fox, these players really knew how to control the bat to place the ball between fielders.

BELOW: *Frankie Frisch*

MOST CAREER SINGLES

PLAYER	SINGLES
Pete Rose	3215
Ty Cobb	3052
Ed Collins	2639
Willie Keeler	2534
Honus Wagner	2426
Rod Carew	2404
Tris Speaker	2383
Nap Lajoie	2354
Cap Anson	2330
Jesse Burkett	2301
Henry Aaron	2294
Ed Rice	2272
Carl Yastrzemski	2262
Stan Musial	2253
Lou Brock	2247
Paul Waner	2243
Frank Frisch	2171
Roger Cramer	2163
Luke Appling	2162
Nellie Fox	2161
Roberto Clemente	2154
Jake Beckley	2142
George Sisler	2122
Richie Ashburn	2119
Luis Aparicio	2108
Zack Wheat	2104
Sam Crawford	2102
Lafayette Cross	2077
Fred Clarke	2061
Al Kaline	2035
Lloyd Waner	2032
Brooks Robinson	2030
Rabbit Maranville	2020
Max Carey	2018
George Van Haltren	2008
George Davis	2007

ABOVE: *Zack Wheat*

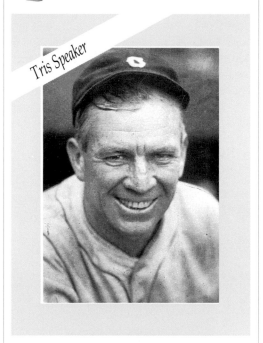

Tris Speaker

Brooks Robinson

Luke Appling

Most Career Doubles

T o hit a double a batter must place the ball between the outfielders. Most times, this means that the ball is hit into the gap with such power that the fielders can't catch up to it. Of course, some runners are so quick that they race to second even if the ball is hit in front of an outfielder. However, most of the elite on the most-doubles list were able to combine longevity with power and speed.

The all-time doubles leader is Tris Speaker, who in his 22-year career led the American League eight times. Finishing in second place is Pete Rose, who hustled his way into second 746 times. The only other member of the 700 or more club are Stan Musial with 725, and Ty Cobb, who ended his career with 724.

Of today's ballplayers, people like Don Mattingly and George Brett are frequently seen cruising into second. Although not known for their speed, they are line-drive hitters who can find those elusive gaps in the outfield.

Frank Robinson

Red Schoendienst

MOST CAREER DOUBLES

PLAYER	DOUBLES
Tris Speaker	793
Pete Rose	746
Stan Musial	725
Ty Cobb	724
Nap Lajoie	652
Honus Wagner	651
Carl Yastrzemski	646
Henry Aaron	624
Paul Waner	605
Charlie Gehringer	574
Harry Heilmann	542
Rogers Hornsby	541
Joe Medwick	540
Al Simmons	539
Lou Gehrig	534
Cap Anson	530
Al Oliver	529
Frank Robinson	528
Ted Williams	525
Willie Mays	523
Joe Cronin	516
Ed Delahanty	508
Babe Ruth	506
Tony Perez	505
Goose Goslin	500
Rusty Staub	499
Ed Rice	498
Al Kaline	498
Heinie Manush	491
Jim Vernon	490
Mel Ott	488
Bill Herman	486
Lou Brock	486
Vada Pinson	485
Brooks Robinson	482
Hal McRae	481
Bill Buckner	480
Zack Wheat	476

Ted Simmons	469
Frank Frisch	466
Jim Bottomley	465
Reggie Jackson	463
Jimmy Foxx	458
Sam Crawford	455
Jake Beckley	455
Jimmy Dykes	453
Joe Morgan	449
Dennis Brouthers	446
George Brett	446
Rod Carew	445
George Burns	444
Richard Bartell	442
George Davis	442
Luke Appling	440
Roberto Clemente	440
Steve Garvey	440
Jim Ryan	439
Ed Collins	437
Joe Sewell	436
Cesar Cedeno	436
Wally Moses	435
Billy Williams	434
Joe Judge	433
Roger Connor	429
Red Schoendienst	427
Sherry Magee	425
George Sisler	425
Willie Stargell	423
Max Carey	419
Orlando Cepeda	417
Bill Dahlen	415
Enos Slaughter	413
Joseph Kuhel	412
Ben Chapman	407
Ernie Banks	407
Cecil Cooper	402
Earl Averill	401
Martin McManus	401
Lafayette Cross	401

BELOW: The all-time doubles mark is 793, held by Tris Speaker.

Most Career Triples

P erhaps the hardest hit to achieve is the triple. Unlike a home run, which just takes power, a triple requires a unique combination of power and speed. The batter is racing around the bases as the outfielders are chasing the bouncing ball. Usually, the outfielder fires the ball to his cutoff man, who relays it into third as the runner slides toward the base. One of baseball's most exciting plays is watching the action on the field as the batter tries to stretch his hit into a triple.

The only player to hit more than 300 triples was Sam Crawford, who wound up with 312 triple-baggers during his playing days. The list includes many players from the 1920s and 1930s, who played in cavernous ballparks like the Polo Grounds and the old Yankee Stadium. With today's modern, smaller parks, it's harder to hit triples. Going down the list, only Stan Musial and Roberto Clemente, of the more contemporary players, made the list.

BELOW: *Sam Crawford displays the style that gave him 312 career triples.*

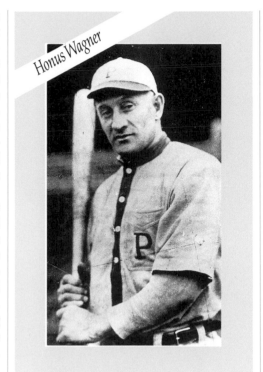

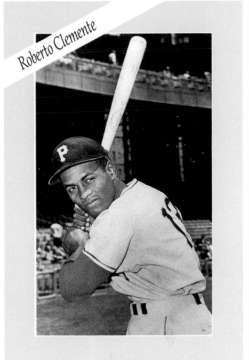

MOST CAREER TRIPLES

PLAYER	TRIPLES
Sam Crawford	312
Ty Cobb	298
Honus Wagner	252
Jake Beckley	246
Roger Connor	227
Tris Speaker	222
Fred Clarke	219
Dennis Brouthers	212
Paul Waner	191
Joe Kelley	189
Ed Collins	186
Jesse Burkett	185
Harry Stovey	185
Ed Rice	184
Ed Delahanty	182
John McPhee	180
Bill Ewing	179
Rabbit Maranville	177
Stan Musial	177
Goose Goslin	173
Zack Wheat	172
Elmer Flick	170
Tommy Leach	170
Rogers Hornsby	169
Joe Jackson	168
Edd Roush	168
George Davis	167
Bill Dahlen	166
Sherry Magee	166
Roberto Clemente	166
Jake Daubert	165
Nap Lajoie	164
George Sisler	164
Pie Traynor	164
Ed Konetchy	163
Lou Gehrig	163
Harry Hooper	160
Heinie Manush	160

Max Carey	159
Joseph Judge	159
Mike Tiernan	159
George Van Haltren	159
Kiki Cuyler	157
Willie Keeler	155
Earle Combs	154
Jimmy Ryan	153
Ed McKean	152
Jim Bottomley	151
Tom Corcoran	151
Harry Heilmann	151

Most Long Hits (Doubles, Triples, and Home Runs)

With all the talk about the lively baseball, some of the players of the game just laugh, because they've been getting production out of the baseball for years. One interesting way to assess a player's worth at the plate is to keep track of his long hits: the homers, triples, and doubles. While singles make up a large part of the game, it is the long blasts that keep the fans coming back for more.

The list of the all-time long hitters begins with the home run king, Hank Aaron. Next on the list is Stan Musial, followed closely by Babe Ruth and Willie Mays. These players, considered by many to be the best to ever play the game, specialized in pounding out those long hits, driving in runs and winning baseball games.

MOST LONG HITS (DOUBLES, TRIPLES, AND HOME RUNS

PLAYER	HITS
Henry Aaron	1477
Stan Musial	1377
Babe Ruth	1356
Willie Mays	1323
Lou Gehrig	1190
Frank Robinson	1186
Carl Yastrzemski	1157
Ty Cobb	1139
Tris Speaker	1132
Jimmy Foxx	1117
Ted Williams	1117
Mel Ott	1071
Reggie Jackson	1045
Pete Rose	1041
Rogers Hornsby	1011
Ernie Banks	1009
Honus Wagner	1004
Al Simmons	995
Al Kaline	972
Tony Perez	963
Willie Stargell	953
Mickey Mantle	952
Billy Williams	948
Eddie Mathews	938
Leon Goslin	921
Willie McCovey	920
Paul Waner	909
Charlie Gehringer	904
Mike Schmidt	904
Nap Lajoie	898
Harmon Killebrew	887
Joe DiMaggio	881
Harry Heilmann	876
Vada Pinson	868
Sam Crawford	862
Joe Medwick	858
Duke Snider	850
Roberto Clemente	846
Rusty Staub	838
Jim Bottomley	835
Al Oliver	825
Orlando Cepeda	823
Brooks Robinson	818
Joe Morgan	813
John Mize	809
Joe Cronin	803

Reggie Jackson

LEFT: *Johnny Mize*

Total Career Bases Leaders

This category, often overlooked, allows the fan to see which player was able to combine all those skills needed to excel at the game of baseball. To find a player's total bases, assign a 4 for homers, a 3 for triples, a 2 for doubles and a 1 for singles and walks. Using this formula, the productive singles hitter can be ranked with home-run sluggers. For instance, Pete Rose, the all-time singles leader, who for this category got 1 point for each single, ranks sixth, just behind Babe Ruth.

The all-time leader in total bases is Hank Aaron, who combined power and speed to accumulate 6,856 total bases. More than 700 total bases behind with 6,134 stands Stan "The Man" Musial, of the St. Louis Cardinals.

TOTAL CAREER BASES LEADERS

PLAYER	BASES
Henry Aaron	6856
Stan Musial	6134
Willie Mays	6066
Ty Cobb	5862
Babe Ruth	5793
Pete Rose	5752
Carl Yastrzemski	5539
Frank Robinson	5373
Tris Speaker	5103
Lou Gehrig	5060
Mel Ott	5041
Jimmy Foxx	4956
Honus Wagner	4888
Ted Williams	4884
Al Kaline	4852
Rogers Hornsby	4712
Ernie Banks	4706
Reggie Jackson	4699
Al Simmons	4685
Billy Williams	4599
Tony Perez	4532
Mickey Mantle	4511
Roberto Clemente	4492
Nap Lajoie	4478
Paul Waner	4478
Eddie Mathews	4349
Sam Crawford	4328
Goose Goslin	4325
Brooks Robinson	4270
Vada Pinson	4264
Ed Collins	4259
Charlie Gehringer	4257
Lou Brock	4238
Willie McCovey	4219
Willie Stargell	4190
Rusty Staub	4185
Cap Anson	4145
Harmon Killebrew	4143
Jake Beckley	4138
Zack Wheat	4100
Al Oliver	4083
Harry Heilmann	4053

ABOVE: *Al Kaline beats the tag to score one of his career 4,852 bases.*

Most Times Struck Out, Nine-Inning Game

S ometimes there's just no place to hide. Everybody strikes out. In fact, some players strike out quite often. But there are those embarrassed few who manage to share the record of having struck out five times in a nine-inning game!

The list includes the great and many lesser-known names. One thing most of these players had in common was their free-swinging style at the plate. Nobody ever cheated Reggie Jackson, Richie Allen, or Frank Howard of their cuts at the plate.

Another point unfortunately has to be made. All of those on this infamous list struck out five times consecutively! Five times they had to return to the dugout to what had to be a quiet reception by their teammates.

MOST TIMES STRUCK OUT NINE-INNING GAME
NATIONAL LEAGUE

PLAYER	TEAM	YEAR	SO
Floyd Young	Pittsburgh	1935	5
Bob Sadowski	Milwaukee	1964	5
Richie Allen	Philadelphia	1964	5
Ron Swoboda	New York	1969	5
Steve Whitaker	San Francisco	1970	5
Richie Allen	St. Louis	1970	5
Bill Russell	Los Angeles	1971	5
Pepe Mangual	Montreal	1975	5
Frank Taveras	New York	1979	5
Dave Kingman	New York	1982	5

AMERICAN LEAGUE

PLAYER	TEAM	YEAR	SO
Lefty Grove	Philadelphia	1933	5
John Broaca	New York	1934	5
Chet Laabs	Detroit	1938	5
Larry Doby	Cleveland	1948	5
Jim Landis	Chicago	1957	5
Bob Allison	Minnesota	1965	5
Reggie Jackson	Oakland	1968	5
Ray Jarvis	Boston	1969	5
Rick Monday	Oakland	1970	5
Frank Howard	Washington	1970	5
Don Buford	Baltimore	1971	5
Rick Manning	Cleveland	1977	5

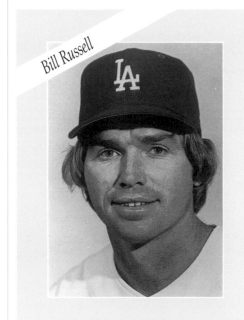

Bill Russell

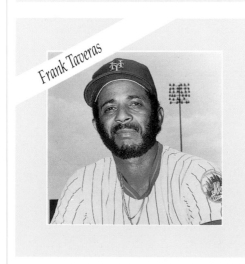

Frank Taveras

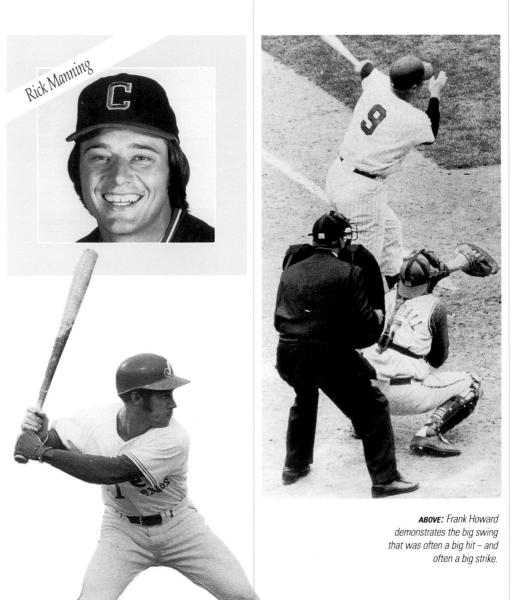

ABOVE: Frank Howard demonstrates the big swing that was often a big hit – and often a big strike.

Rick Manning

RIGHT: Pepe Mangual

Most Times Struck Out in an Extra-Inning Game

Perhaps the longest trip in baseball for a batter is the journey back to the dugout after being struck out. Nobody likes to go down swinging and then take the abuse of the fans for having failed. Most of the game's career strikeout leaders are free-swinging long-ball hitters, who sacrifice batting average for the chance of popping one over the wall. Surprisingly, however, the leaders in most times struck out in a single game are not necessarily known for their deep threat.

With a few exceptions, like Reggie Jackson and Richie Allen, the players on this list just had a bad day. To make this infamous list you have to have ample times at bat. Even the worst hitter in the game can't strike out five times in only four at bats. Therefore, you'll note that a good number of these players unluckily got to set their record during an extra-inning ballgame.

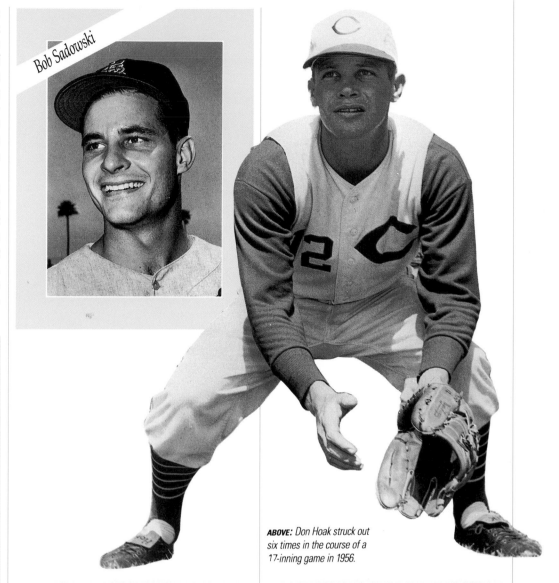

Bob Sadowski

ABOVE: Don Hoak struck out six times in the course of a 17-inning game in 1956.

Billy Cowan

BELOW: Cecil Cooper

MOST TIMES STRUCK OUT IN AN EXTRA-INNING GAME

AMERICAN LEAGUE

PLAYER	TEAM	YEAR	INNINGS	SO
Carl Weilman	St. Louis	1913	15	6
Rick Reichardt	California	1966	17	6
Billy Cowan	California	1971	20	6
Cecil Cooper	Boston	1974	15	6
Donie Bush	Detroit	1910	10	5
Ray Morgan	Washington	1911	10	5
Scott Perry	Philadelphia	1918	11	5
Ossie Bluege	Washington	1923	11	5
Lefty Grove	Philadelphia	1933	11	5
Johnny Broaca	New York	1934	11	5
Chet Laabs	Detroit	1938	11	5
Lary Doby	Cleveland	1948	11	5
Jim Landis	Chicago	1957	11	5
Bob Allison	Minnesota	1965	11	5
Sandy Valdespino	Minnesota	1967	20	5
Ray Jarvis	Boston	1969	20	5
Reggie Jackson	Oakland	1968	20	5
Rick Monday	Oakland	1970	20	5
Frank Howard	Washington	1970	20	5
Don Buford	Baltimore	1971	20	5
Bobby Darwin	Minnesota	1972	22	5
Roy Smalley	Minnesota	1976	17	5
Rick Manning	Cleveland	1977	17	5
Kevin Bell	Chicago	1980	17	5

NATIONAL LEAGUE

PLAYER	TEAM	YEAR	INNINGS	SO
Don Hoak	Chicago	1956	17	6
Oscar Walker	Buffalo	1879	17	5
Harry Stovey	Boston	1891	10	5
Pete Dowling	Louisville	1899	10	5
Benny Kauf	New York	1918	14	5
Les Bell	St. Louis	1927	11	5
Pep Young	Pittsburgh	1935	11	5
Dee Fondy	Chicago	1953	11	5
Steve Bilko	St. Louis	1953	10	5
Jackie Robinson	Brooklyn	1953	10	5
Bob Sadowski	Milwaukee	1964	10	5
Richie Allen	Philadelphia	1964	10	5
Ron Swoboda	New York	1969	10	5
Steve Whitaker	San Francisco	1970	10	5
Richie Allen	St. Louis	1970	10	5
Bill Russell	Los Angeles	1971	10	5
Pepe Mangual	Montreal	1975	10	5
Frank Taveras	New York	1979	10	5

Most Times Struck Out, Career

S ometimes when a batter takes a big swing, he ends up with a big whiff. The list of the game's all-time strikeout leaders not surprisingly includes some of the game's greatest home-run hitters. At the head of the pack is Reggie Jackson, who finished the 1987 season having fanned a record 2,597 times. Some of the other home-run champs who also made this infamous list include Willie Stargell, Mike Schmidt, Mickey Mantle, Willie Mays, and Ron Santo.

Perhaps the biggest surprise is the absence of the legendary Sultan of Swat, the Babe himself. Although Ruth finished his career with 714 home runs, he made contact often enough to be excluded from this list.

MOST TIMES STRUCK OUT, CAREER	
PLAYER	STRIKEOUTS
Reggie Jackson	2,597
Willie Stargell	1,936
Tony Perez	1,867
Mike Schmidt	1,824
Dave Kingman	1,816
Bobby Bonds	1,757
Lou Brock	1,730
Mickey Mantle	1,710
Harmon Killebrew	1,699
Lee May	1,570
Dick Allen	1,556
Willie McCovey	1,550
Frank Robinson	1,532
Willie Mays	1,526
Rick Monday	1,513
Greg Luzinski	1,495
Eddie Mathews	1,487
Frank Howard	1,460
Jim Wynn	1,427
George Scott	1,418
George Foster	1,418
Carl Yastrzemski	1,393
Dwight Evans	1,387
Hank Aaron	1,383
Ron Santo	1,343

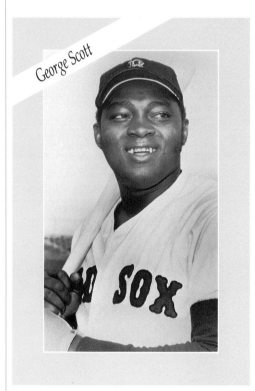

George Scott

Mike Schmidt

Easiest to Strike Out, Career

O f course, the easiest players to strike out have been those who go for the long ball. To hit a homer in the big leagues takes a powerful swing. To generate the requisite power, most home-run sluggers are free swinging, putting all their energy into the motion of the bat. To get this power, they sacrifice accuracy, leading in many cases to a strikeout.

From Mickey Mantle to Mike Schmidt, the names of those players who constantly lead the league in homers also seem to top the list in strikeouts. Surprisingly, record-setters Hank Aaron, Babe Ruth, and Roger Maris don't even make the top 20 of those easy strikeout victims. That means for the most part, these three, if they weren't hitting it out of the park, at least made contact with the ball!

RIGHT: The easiest strikeout in the big leagues was Dave Nicholson, with a ratio of 2.48.

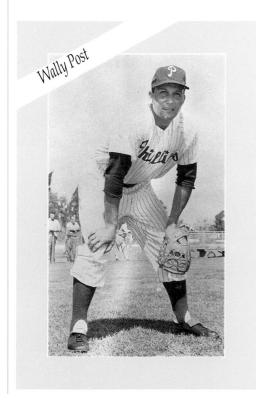

Wally Post

Larry Doby

Richie Allen

EASIEST TO STRIKE OUT, CAREER

PLAYER	YEARS	AT-BATS	STRIKEOUTS	RATIO
Dave Nicholson	7	1,419	573	2.48
Dave Kingman	10	3,839	1,139	3.37
Mike Schmidt	9	4,261	1,077	3.96
Reggie Jackson	14	6,863	1,728	3.97
Bobby Bonds	13	6,880	1,713	4.02
Richie Allen	15	6,332	1,556	4.07
Donn Clendenon	12	4,648	1,140	4.08
Rick Monday	15	5,572	1,362	4.09
Willie Stargell	19	7,794	1,903	4.10
Woodie Held	14	4,019	944	4.25
Frank Howard	16	6,488	1,460	4.44
Deron Johnson	15	5,940	1,318	4.51
Jimmy Wynn	16	6,653	1,427	4.66
Mickey Mantle	18	8,102	1,710	4.73
Harmon Killebrew	22	8,147	1,699	4.80
Lee May	16	7,463	1,538	4.85
Bob Allison	13	5,032	1,033	4.87
Doug Rader	11	5,186	1,057	4.90
Wally Post	15	4,007	813	4.92
Tony Perez	17	8,503	1,628	5.22
George Scott	14	7,433	1,418	5.24
Larry Doby	13	5,348	1,011	5.29
Willie McCovey	22	8,197	1,550	5.29
Boog Powell	17	6,681	1,226	5.45
Eddie Mathews	17	8,537	1,487	5.74
Lou Brock	19	10,332	1,730	5.97

Hardest to Strike Out, Career

W hile the symbol of pure perfection for the pitcher is the strikeout, the comparable sign for the batter is the home run. Therefore, it shouldn't come as a shock that the game's hardest-to-strike-out players are those who concentrated on meeting the ball instead of clobbering it over the fence. Those players who choke up on the bat and strike to send the ball for line-drive base hits have proven to be the toughest to strike out.

Looking at the names and the statistics, we see that the hardest players to strike out, players like Lloyd Waner and Nellie Fox, averaged fewer than 10 homers a year. On the other hand, big swingers like Reggie Jackson and Dave Kingman are known as much for their strikeouts as their home runs. They walk dejectedly back to the dugout almost as often as they triumphantly trot around the bases.

HARDEST TO STRIKE OUT, CAREER				
PLAYER	YEARS	AT-BATS	STRIKEOUTS	RATIO
Joe Sewell	14	7,132	114	62.6
Lloyd Waner	18	7,772	173	44.9
Nellie Fox	19	9,232	216	42.7
Tommy Holmes	11	4,992	122	40.9
Andy High	13	4,400	130	33.8
Sam Rice	20	9,269	275	33.7
Frankie Frisch	19	9,112	272	33.5
Don Mueller	12	4,364	146	29.9

RIGHT: *Sam Rice (center), shown here on a golf outing with Jess Petty (left) and Al Simmons (right), was very tough to strike out.*

ABOVE: *Nellie Fox was the third-hardest batter to strike out in baseball history.*

Hardest to Double Up, Career

No ballplayer likes to hit into the dreaded double play. Besides being a rally-stopper, the double play means that you've failed either to advance the runner or get the run batted in.

Those players who most often hit into double plays are usually slow of foot. In the course of the game, some players have distinguished themselves by being able to avoid the double play. Opposing managers fear these hitters, because more often than not if they get the ball in play, runners wind up in scoring position or cross the plate.

Not surprisingly, besides being fast, many of the players on the hardest-to-double-up list bat from the left, giving them an edge in getting to first base. One of the hardest players ever to double up was Don Buford. During his ten years in the majors, Buford came to bat 4,553 times and hit into only 33 double plays!

HARDEST TO DOUBLE UP, CAREER

PLAYER	AT-BATS	DOUBLE PLAYS	RATIO
Don Buford	4,553	33	138
Don Blasingame	5,296	43	123
Mickey Rivers	4,540	38	119
Richie Ashburn	8,365	85	98
Joe Morgan	7,737	80	97
George Case	3,964	42	94
Vic Davalillo	4,017	43	93
Lou Brock	10,332	14	91
Stan Hack	7,100	78	91
Bill Nicholson	5,534	61	91
Bud Harrelson	4,744	53	90
Arky Vaughan	6,125	70	88
Rick Monday	5.571	65	86
Del Unser	5,142	60	86
Bert Campaneris	8,459	102	83
Bill Bruton	6,065	73	83
Augie Galan	5,937	72	82
Maury Wills	7,588	92	82
Sandy Alomar	4,780	58	82
Dick McAuliffe	6,185	77	80

RIGHT: One of the hardest players ever to double up is Mickey Rivers. In 4,540 at-bats, Rivers hit into only 38 DPs.

Most Times Walked in a Game

One way to get on base is to draw a walk from the pitcher. The term "walk" probably comes from the fact that getting the umpire to call ball four allows the player to walk to first base, instead of having to run out a hit. Some players have a real talent for getting walks. You'll find that those with the most walks are generally considered to have good judgement at the plate. A prime example is Keith Hernandez of the New York Mets, who always seems to be in the top ten in bases on balls.

It takes a lot of patience and pitch selection to get a walk. Some players can purposefully foul off close pitches and take the balls until they work that free pass from the pitcher. Of course, some of the game's long-ball sluggers, like Jimmy Foxx, got a lot of intentional walks because pitchers decided to give them the base and work at getting the next man out instead.

Bobby Grich

BELOW: Rodney Scott

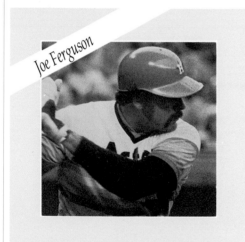

Joe Ferguson

Tim Foli

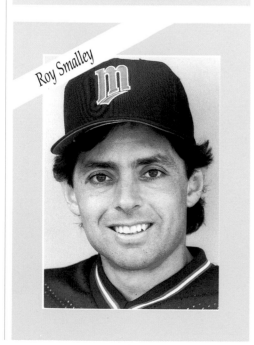

Roy Smalley

MOST TIMES WALKED IN A GAME
AMERICAN LEAGUE

PLAYER	TEAM	YEAR	WALKS
Jimmy Foxx	Boston	1938	6
Sammy Strang	Chicago	1902	5
Elmer Flick	Cleveland	1902	5
Kid Elberfeld	Detroit	1902	5
Charlie Hemphill	New York	1911	5
Tris Speaker	Boston	1912	5
Roger Peckinpaugh	New York	1919	5
Whitey Witt	New York	1924	5
Ira Flagstead	Boston	1925	5
Max Bishop	Philadelphia	1929	5
Max Bishop	Philadelphia	1930	5
Earl Averill	Cleveland	1932	5
Jo-Jo White	Detroit	1935	5
Lou Gehrig	New York	1935	5
Ben Chapman	New York	1936	5
Billy Rogell	Detroit	1938	5
Hersh Martin	New York	1945	5
Larry Doby	Cleveland	1951	5
Bobby Grich	Baltimore	1975	5
Roy Smalley	Minnesota	1978	5

NATIONAL LEAGUE

PLAYER	TEAM	YEAR	WALKS
Walt Wilmot	Chicago	1891	6
Fred Carroll	Pittsburgh	1889	5
Pop Smith	Boston	1890	5
Kip Selbach	Cincinnati	1899	5
Sam Mertes	New York	1903	5
Heinie Groh	New York	1922	5
Hughie Critz	Cincinnati	1928	5
Mel Ott	New York	1929	5
Gus Suhr	Pittsburgh	1930	5
Mel Ott	New York	1933	5
Mel Ott	New York	1943	5
Mel Ott	New York	1944	5
Max West	Pittsburgh	1948	5
Solly Hemus	St. Louis	1951	5
Andy Seminick	Philadelphia	1951	5
Richie Allen	Philadelphia	1968	5
Ellie Hendricks	Chicago	1972	5
Tim Foli	Montreal	1973	5
Joe Ferguson	Houston	1978	5
Johnny Bench	Cincinnati	1979	5
Rod Scott	Montreal	1980	5

Most Career Bases on Balls

S tanding at the plate, getting ready to pounce on the pitch, few batters think about drawing a walk. Yet since four balls equals a walk, many batters get that free ride to first base. Perhaps it's unfair to refer to a walk as a free ride, since so many players are adept at getting the base on balls. As the old saying goes, a walk is as good as a hit.

Many pitchers, fearing that the batter is a threat at the plate, pitch around the hitter. Therefore, such sluggers as Babe Ruth and Mickey Mantle got few pitches in the strike zone to smack. Other great players, like Ted Williams and Joe Morgan, were known for having a keen hitting eye. For these players the umpire sometimes gave them the benefit of the doubt for pitches close to the strike zone.

The list of the leaders in this category include a fine mixture of home-run sluggers and finesse players. From the Babe to Al Kaline, these ballplayers sometimes got to first base without ever swinging the bat!

MOST CAREER BASES ON BALLS

PLAYER	BB
Babe Ruth	2056
Ted Williams	2019
Joe Morgan	1865
Carl Yastrzemski	1845
Mickey Mantle	1734
Mel Ott	1708
Ed Yost	1614
Stan Musial	1599
Pete Rose	1566
Harmon Killebrew	1559
Lou Gehrig	1508
Darrell Evans	1480
Willie Mays	1464
Jimmy Foxx	1452
Eddie Mathews	1444
Mike Schmidt	1437
Frank Robinson	1420
Henry Aaron	1402
Reggie Jackson	1376
Willie McCovey	1345
Luke Appling	1302
Al Kaline	1277
Ken Singleton	1262
Rusty Staub	1255
Jimmy Wynn	1224
Ed Collins	1213
Pee Wee Reese	1210
Richie Ashburn	1198
Charlie Gehringer	1185
Max Bishop	1153
Toby Harrah	1153
Tris Speaker	1146
Ron Santo	1108
Lu Blue	1092
Stan Hack	1092
Paul Waner	1091
Bobby Grich	1087
Graig Nettles	1079
Bob Johnson	1073
Harlond B. Clift	1070
Joe Cronin	1059
Ron Fairly	1052
Billy Williams	1045
Norm Cash	1043
Eddie Joost	1041
Max Carey	1040
Rogers Hornsby	1038
Jim Gilliam	1036
Sal Bando	1031
Enos Slaughter	1018
Rod Carew	1018
Ralph Kiner	1011
John Powell	1001

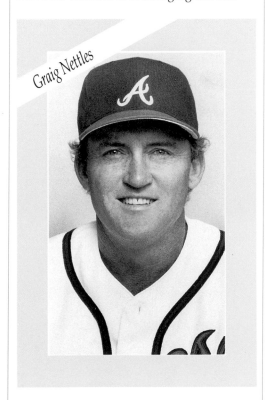

Graig Nettles

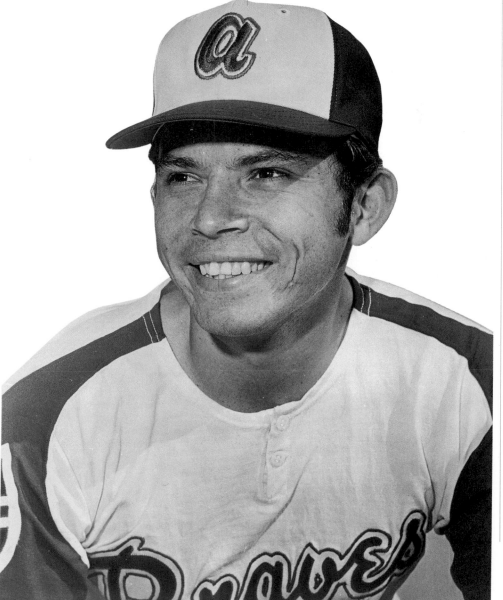

RIGHT: *Darrel Evans*

Most Career Hit by Pitch

N obody actually looks forward to getting hit by a pitch. A fastball traveling in excess of 90 miles per hour can leave quite a bruise. Yet some players really have a knack for "taking one for the team." Since the object of the game is to get on base to score runs, players who often get hit by a pitch tend to have high on-base percentages.

During the 1987 season, Don Baylor was hit by a pitch 32 times and thus became the career leader in getting nicked. The trick, of course, is to make an effort to get out of the way so that the baseball just glances off your uniform. Some of the players on this list wore baggy shirts to give a bigger target for the pitcher.

The National League hit-by-pitch champion is Ron Hunt. During his 12-year career with the Mets, Dodgers, Giants, and Expos, Hunt managed to get hit 243 times in 1,483 games played.

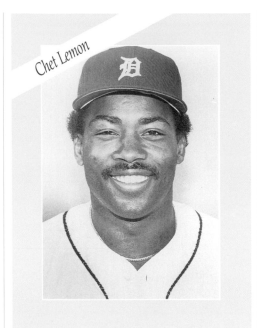

Chet Lemon

MOST CAREER HIT BY PITCH		
PLAYER	GAMES	TIMES HIT
Don Baylor	2200	259
Ron Hunt	1483	243
Frank Robinson	2808	198
Minnie Minoso	1841	192
Nellie Fox	2367	142
Art Fletcher	1529	141
Chet Lemon	1613	132
Carlton Fisk	1962	119
Sherm Lollar	1752	115
Buck Herzog	1493	114
Frank Crosetti	1682	114
Bill Freehan	1774	114

BELOW: *Ron Hunt*

RIGHT: *The indestructible Don Baylor leads the list of most career hit by pitch.*

Most Times Faced Pitcher, No Official At-Bats

S ome of the statistics of the game are very complicated. For instance, when calculating at-bats, walks, hit by pitch, sacrifice hits, and sacrifice flies aren't counted. So if you wa. a real tricky trivia question, ask the most avid baseball fan to name any player who went to the plate six times yet wasn't credited with an official at-bat.

Give up? A total of five players have claimed that distinction. In the American League, Jimmy Foxx went to the plate six times on June 16, 1938 and drew six bases on balls. In the National League, Charles Smith, Walter Wilmot, Mike Huggins, and Bill Urbanski all accomplished this quirky feat.

MOST TIMES FACED PITCHER, NO OFFICAL AT-BATS

PLAYER	AT-BATS	TEAM	DESCRIPTION	DATE
Charlie Smith	6	Boston NL	5 walks, 1 hit by pitcher	17 Apr 1890
Walter Wilmot	6	Chicago NL	6 walks	22 Aug 1891
Miller Huggins	6	St. Louis NL	4 walks, 1 sacrifice hit, 1 sacrifice fly	1 June 1910
Bill Urbanski	6	Boston NL	4 walks, 2 sacrifice hits	13 June 1934
Jimmy Foxx	6	Boston AL	6 walks	16 June 1938

RIGHT: *Jimmy Foxx*

LEFT: *Miller Huggins is one of the few men to hold the quirky record of facing a pitcher six times with no official at-bats.*

Most Stolen Bases in a Season

T he speed demons are stealing the game. With the advent of artificial turf, baseball teams rely heavily on these swift denizens of the basepaths. Defensively, outfielders must be able to dash to the gaps to cut off baseballs bounding on the slick rug.

Offensively, these same track stars show off their talents by burning up the basepaths. Willie Wilson, Tim Raines, Vince Coleman, and Eric Davis routinely swipe the extra base. But the master of them all is Rickey Henderson of the New York Yankees. In 1982, while a member of the Oakland A's, Henderson stole a major-league record 130 bases!

Vince Coleman set a rookie record for stolen bases when he "stole" the hearts of St. Louis Cardinals fans by snatching 110 bases. Coleman broke Juan Samuel's previous rookie mark of 72 by stealing third and then home on the same pitch!

BELOW: Tim Raines

RIGHT: Maury Wills was the first player to steal more than 100 bases in a season. Here he swipes his 104th of the 1962 season.

MOST STOLEN BASES IN A SEASON

PLAYER	YEAR	SB
Rickey Henderson	1982	130
Lou Brock	1974	118
Rickey Henderson	1983	108
Maury Wills	1962	104
Rickey Henderson	1980	100
Ron LeFlore	1980	97
Ty Cobb	1915	96
Omar Moreno	1980	96
Maury Wills	1965	94
Tim Raines	1983	90
Clyde Milan	1912	88
Willie Wilson	1979	83
Ty Cobb	1911	83
Bob Bescher	1911	81
Eddie Collins	1910	81
Dave Collins	1980	79
Willie Wilson	1980	79
Ron LeFlore	1979	78
Tim Raines	1982	78

Willie Wilson

Ron LeFlore

Most Stolen Bases, Career

fleet-footed ballplayer can be a magician on the basepaths, turning singles into doubles and doubles into three-baggers. In the modern game, these swift base-stealers, known as "rabbits," can be so devastating to a pitcher's concentration as to disrupt the whole game. When a Rickey Henderson or Vince Coleman gets on base, the fun begins. Infielders nervously await the dash toward second. The pitcher has to make three or four tosses over to first just to keep the base runner honest. The batter, knowing that in all probability the pitcher must hurl a fastball to give his catcher a chance to make a throw, grips the bat handle waiting for that fat pitch.

The all-time stolen base leader is Lou Brock of the St. Louis Cardinals, who racked up 938 thefts. Stealing the base has become such as science that Brock's record will probably be shattered by a Coleman or a Henderson. Tim Raines of the Montreal Expos had a physicist calculate that if he gets a certain lead off the base, his speed makes it virtually impossible for any catcher to relay a throw to second in time to get him out!

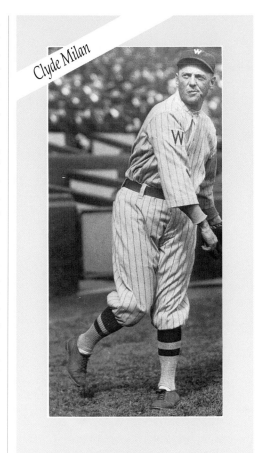

Clyde Milan

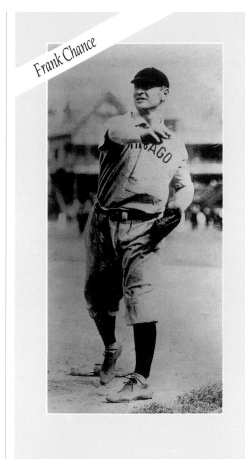

Frank Chance

MOST STOLEN BASES, CAREER

PLAYER	STEALS
Lou Brock	938
Ty Cobb	892
Eddie Collins	743
Max Carey	738
Honus Wagner	703
Rickey Henderson	701
Joe Morgan	689
Bert Campaneris	631
Maury Wills	586
Davey Lopes	557
Cesar Cedeno	550
Willie Wilson	529
Tim Raines	511
Luis Aparicio	506
Clyde Milan	495
Omar Moreno	487
Jimmy Sheckard	474
Bobby Bonds	461
Ron LeFlore	455
Sherry McGee	441
Tris Speaker	433
Bob Beecher	428
Frankie Frisch	419
Tommy Harper	408
Frank Chance	405
Donie Bush	405

BELOW: *Donie Bush (left) and Roger Peckinpaugh.*

Stealing Second, Third and Home in One Game

No catcher likes a runner to steal a base. So imagine the embarrassment of having a runner steal second, third, and home during his times on base in a game. Some stolen bases can be blamed on the pitcher's inability to keep the runner close, but to the fans, it's the catcher's job to nail these felons.

If a runner really wanted to show up a catcher and exhibit his speed, how about stealing second, third, and home in one inning! That's what Ty Cobb was able to accomplish three times in his career, in addition to thrice stealing all three in one game. In one memorable game, Cobb stole the bases on three consecutive pitches. One minute he was standing on first base and three pitches later, he was sliding home with his spikes flying, swiping the base!

Rod Carew

Dave Nelson

BELOW: *Three times in his memorable career Ty Cobb stole second, third, and home in one game.*

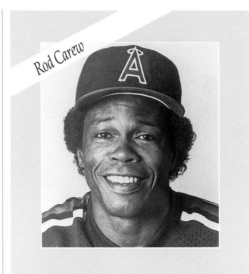

STEALING SECOND, THIRD, AND HOME IN ONE GAME

AMERICAN LEAGUE

PLAYER	TEAM	YEAR
Dave Fultz	PHI	1902
Wild Bill Donovan	DET	1906
Bill Coughlin	DET	1906
Ty Cobb	DET	1907
Ty Cobb	DET	1909
Ty Cobb	DET	1911
Ty Cobb	DET	1912
Joe Jackson	CLE	1912
Eddie Collins	PHI	1912
Eddie Ainsmith	WAS	1913
Red Faber	CHI	1915
Danny Moeller	WAS	1915
Fritz Maisel	NY	1915
Ty Cobb	DET	1917
Buck Weaver	CHI	1919
Braggo Roth	WAS	1920
Ty Cobb	DET	1924
Bob Meusel	NY	1927
Jackie Tavener	DET	1927
Jackie Tavener	DET	1928
Don Kolloway	CHI	1941
Rod Carew	MIN	1969
Dave Nelson	TEX	1974

NATIONAL LEAGUE

PLAYER	TEAM	YEAR
Honus Wagner	PIT	1902
Honus Wagner	PIT	1907
Buck Herzog	NY	1908
Hans Lobert	CIN	1908
Honus Wagner	PIT	1909
Bill O'Hara	NY	1909
Dode Paskert	CIN	1910
Wilbur Good	CHI	1915
Jimmy Johnston	BKN	1916
Greasy Neale	CIN	1919
Max Carey	PIT	1923
Max Carey	PIT	1925
Harvey Hendrick	BKN	1928
Jackie Robinson	BKN	1954
Pete Rose	PHI	1980

Most Career Steals of Home

S tealing home plate takes a combination of speed, cunning, and a little bit of luck. Unlike trying to steal second or third, a dash toward home plate requires no throw from the catcher. Instead, the pitcher throws toward the plate as the runner barrels home. The catcher gets the pitch, spins toward third and in that cloud of dirt and sand, tries to tag the runner out.

The all-time leader in stealing home is Ty Cobb. A master of the stolen base, Cobb swiped home a record 35 times. One of the last of the nitty-gritty ballplayers, Cobb was notorious for filing down his cleats so that they were razor-sharp. Sliding feet first, Cobb used those spikes as a lethal weapon.

Speed alone is not enough when a runner takes off for home. The all-time total stolen base leader, Lou Brock, never stole home, despite his record 938 steals!

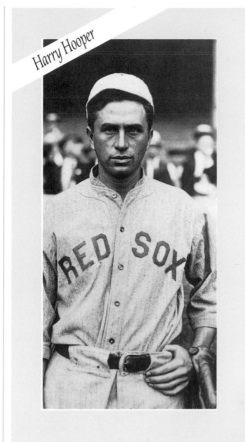

Harry Hooper

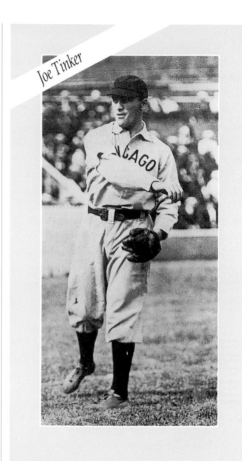

Joe Tinker

MOST CAREER STEALS OF HOME

PLAYER	STEALS
Ty Cobb	35
George Burns	27
Wildfire Schulte	22
Johnny Evers	21
Jackie Robinson	19
Frankie Frisch	19
George Sisler	19
Jimmy Sheckard	18
Eddie Collins	17
Joe Tinker	17
Larry Doyle	17
Rod Carew	16
Lou Gehrig	15
Tris Speaker	15
Ben Chapman	14
Max Carey	14
Fritz Maisel	14
Vic Saier	14
Honus Wagner	14
Heinie Zimmerman	13
Harry Hooper	11
Fred Merkle	11
George Moriarty	11
Braggo Roth	11
Shano Collins	10
Buck Herzog	10
Jimmy Johnston	10
Babe Ruth	10
Bill Werber	10
Ross Youngs	10

LEFT: *Johnny Evers stole home 21 times in his career.*

Most Consecutive Games Scoring One or More Runs

S ometimes the runs come in bunches. For some players, those bunches can extend over a few games. As if suddenly blessed, some ballplayers will put together a string of games where they cross home plate at least once.

The American League record is held by Robert Rolfe of the New York Yankees, who scored a run in 18 consecutive games, from August 9, 1939 through the second game on August 25. During that stretch, Rolfe scored a total of 30 runs.

Since 1900, Ted Kluszewski of the Cincinnati Reds holds the National League record of 17. The "Big Klu's" streak started on August 17, 1954 and ran through September 13, by which time he had crossed home plate a total of 24 times.

MOST CONSECUTIVE GAMES SCORING ONE OR MORE RUNS

GAMES	RUNS	PLAYER	TEAM	DATES
24	35	Bill Hamilton	Philadelphia NL	6 July – 2 Aug 1894
18	30	Robert Rolfe	New York AL	9 Aug – 25 Aug 1939
17	24	Ted Kluszewski	Cincinnati NL	27 Aug – 13 Sep 1954

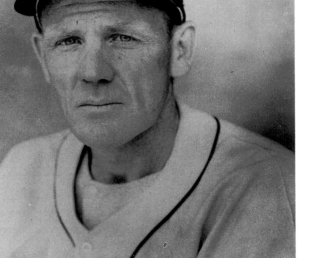

LEFT: In 1939 Robert Rolfe scored 30 times in 18 consecutive games.

RIGHT: Bill Hamilton scored one or more runs in 24 consecutive games in 1894.

LEFT: Big Ted Kluszewski trails Hamilton and Rolfe, scoring only 24 times in 17 straight games.

Most Runs Scored in a Season

S ome players have really made it a habit of crossing home plate. Having the dexterity and luck to get the hits, or the eye to draw walks, these players often are in the position to be driven home by their teammates. Others have the speed to steal that extra base and fly home on singles to the outfield.

Since 1900, the leader in runs scored for a single season is Chuck Klein of the 1930 Philadelphia Phillies. Klein raced home 158 times during that memorable year. Over in the American League, Babe Ruth holds the highwater mark. The great Yankee slugger, who also knew how to work the base on balls, took that rather hefty body of his around home a remarkable 177 times during the 1921 season. Recently, another Yankee superstar, Rickey Henderson, has made it a habit of leading the league in runs scored.

MOST RUNS SCORED IN A SEASON

PLAYER	RUNS	GAMES	TEAM	YEAR
Billy Hamilton	196	131	Philadelphia NL	1894
Babe Ruth	177	152	New York AL	1921
Chuck Klein	158	156	Philadelphia NL	1930

RIGHT: *Babe Ruth played himself in* Pride of the Yankees, *a film about Lou Gehrig. The Babe is one of three players to hold the record for most runs scored in a season.*

Most Career Runs Scored

To get on the most-runs-scored list a ball-player must have had many opportunities to get on base, allowing the men behind to drive him in. Not surprisingly, most of these players had long careers, and a good many of them played on successful teams. Baseball is so much a team sport that some of the individual records really reflect a joint effort. Runs scored is a perfect example. You could have had the league's highest on-base percentage and still not make the list if the players batting behind you couldn't get the hit to drive you in.

Babe Ruth scored 2,174 career runs to make the list. Ruth played on the high-scoring New York Yankees during the 1920s and 1930s. Ruth led the American League in runs scored eight times during that period.

The name on top of the list belongs to Ty Cobb. Cobb crossed home plate 2,245 times. Cobb enhanced his chances of scoring with his swift feet, swiping plenty of extra bases to set up the run.

BELOW: *Ted Williams*

RIGHT: *Babe Ruth (left) and William Bendix, who portrayed him in* The Babe Ruth Story. *In his career Ruth scored 2,174 runs.*

MOST CAREER RUNS SCORED

PLAYER	RUNS SCORED
Ty Cobb	2,245
Babe Ruth	2,174
Henry Aaron	2,174
Pete Rose	2,165
Willie Mays	2,062
Stan Musial	1,949
Lou Gehrig	1,888
Tris Speaker	1,881
Mel Ott	1,859
Frank Robinson	1,829
Ed Collins	1,816
Carl Yastrzemski	1,816
Ted Williams	1,798
Charlie Gehringer	1,774
Jimmy Foxx	1,751
Honus Wagner	1,740
Willie Keeler	1,720
Cap Anson	1,712
Jesse Burkett	1,708
Bill Hamilton	1,690
Mickey Mantle	1,677
John McPhee	1,674
George Van Haltren	1,650
Joe Morgan	1,650
Jimmy Ryan	1,640
Paul Waner	1,627
Al Kaline	1,622
Fred Clarke	1,620
Lou Brock	1,610
Roger Connor	1,607
Jake Beckley	1,601
Ed Delahanty	1,596
Bill Dahlen	1,594
Rogers Hornsby	1,579
Reggie Jackson	1,551
George Davis	1,546
Max Carey	1,545
Hugh Duffy	1,545
Frankie Frisch	1,532
Ed Rice	1,514
Eddie Mathews	1,509
Tom Brown	1,507
Dennis Brouthers	1,507
Al Simmons	1,507
Nap Lajoie	1,506

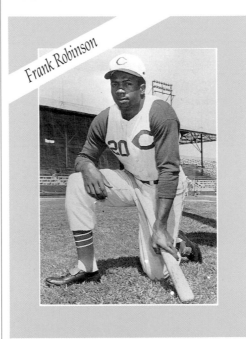

Frank Robinson

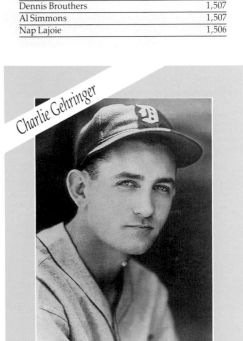

Charlie Gehringer

Most Games Started, Career

With all the mechanics necessary to be a successful pitcher in the big leagues, the body must be put through a tortuous test. Not only is a tremendous strain put on the arm, but the legs and back take a pounding too. Couple this with the fact that the minor leagues are loaded with pitchers hungry for a chance to start in the big time and you begin to realize just how special are the pitchers on this list.

The man who was given the ball to start more often than anyone else was Denton True Young. Better known as Cy, he was such a great pitcher that they named an award after him. Cy Young started 818 games in the major leagues.

The players on this list got the starting call every four or five days during their careers. Of today's ball players, some of the pitchers have made it to the top of the list. Still active, Don Sutton, Phil Niekro, and Tommy John get out there and compete with players who weren't even born when they started pitching in the majors.

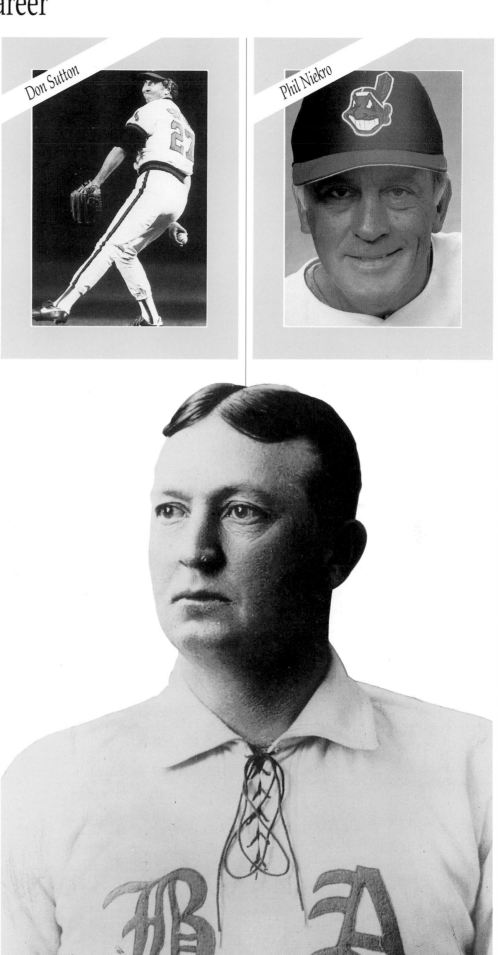

MOST GAMES STARTED, CAREER

PITCHER	GAMES
Cy Young	818
Don Sutton	706
Gaylord Perry	690
Phil Niekro	690
Steve Carlton	687
Jim Galvin	682
Walter Johnson	666
Warren Spahn	665
Tom Seaver	647
Jim Kaat	625
Tommy John	614
Early Wynn	612
Robin Roberts	609
Grover Alexander	598
Ferguson Jenkins	594
Tim Keefe	593
Nolan Ryan	577
Kid Nichols	561
Eppa Rixey	552
Christy Mathewson	551
Mike Welch	549
Red Ruffing	536
Bert Blyleven	535
Jerry Koosman	527
Jim Palmer	521
Jim Bunning	519
John Clarkson	518
John Powell	517
Tony Mullane	505
Gus Weyhing	503
Old Hoss Radbourn	503

RIGHT: The leader by far in games started is Cy Young.

Most Games Pitched, Career

The way some pitchers are used it's amazing their arms don't fall off. There are many ways to measure a pitcher's success. One basic method is to see how many games he pitched in a career. Of course, with the growth of the relief pitcher, players now tend to have longer careers. Starting pitchers don't burn out as quickly, since few of them ever have to complete the game. Most teams carry two or even three relief aces to take the pressure off the starting staff.

The all-time record-holder for most games pitched is Hoyt Wilhelm. During his 21-year career, Wilhelm pitched in 1,070 games. Of those games, Wilhelm started only 52 times.

This statistic may be a little skewed since it's hard to distinguish between the starters and the relievers. Regardless of their status, it is true to say these players had to be ready to pitch every time they were given the ball.

RIGHT: *In a career that spanned 21 years Hoyt Wilhelm pitched 1,070 games.*

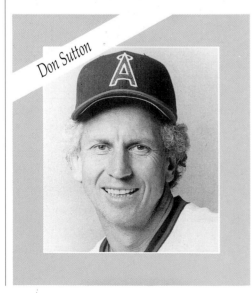
Don Sutton

Rollie Fingers

RIGHT: *Lindy McDaniel*

MOST GAMES PITCHED, CAREER

PITCHER	YEARS	GAMES
Hoyt Wilhelm	21	1070
Lindy McDaniel	21	987
Rollie Fingers	17	944
Kent Tekulve	14	943
Cy Young	22	906
Sparky Lyle	16	899
Jim Kaat	25	898
Don McMahon	18	874
Phil Niekro	24	863
Roy Face	16	848
Gene Garber	17	843
Frank McGraw	19	824
Walter Johnson	21	802
Gaylord Perry	22	777
Darold Knowles	16	765
Goose Gossage	16	765
Don Sutton	22	758
Ron Reed	19	751
Warren Spahn	21	750
Tom Burgmeier	17	745
Ron Perranoski	13	737
Steve Carlton	23	737
Ron Kline	17	736
Clay Carroll	15	731
Mike Marshall	14	723
Gary Lavelle	12	716
John Klippstein	18	711
Stu Miller	16	704
Tommy John	24	704
Pud Galvin	14	697
Joe Niekro	21	697
Grover Alexander	20	696
Bob Miller	17	694
Bill Campbell	14	693
Eppa Rixey	21	692
Grant Jackson	18	692
Early Wynn	23	691
Eddie Fisher	15	690
Ted Abernathy	14	681
Robin Roberts	19	676
Waite Hoyt	21	675
Red Faber	20	669
Dave Giusti	15	668
Jack Quinn	21	665
Ferguson Jenkins	19	664
Tom Seaver	20	656
Paul Lindblad	14	655
Wilbur Wood	18	651
Charlie Hough	18	649
Sam Jones	22	647
Dave LaRoche	14	647
Nolan Ryan	21	645
Dutch Leonard	20	640
Gerry Staley	15	640
Diego Segui	15	639
Christy Mathewson	17	635
Charlie Root	17	632
Jim Perry	17	630
Lew Burdette	18	626
Murry Dickson	18	625
Woody Fryman	18	625
Red Ruffing	22	624
Bruce Sutter	11	623
Charlie Nichols	15	620
Dick Tidrow	13	620
Herb Pennock	22	617
Lefty Grove	17	616
Burleigh Grimes	19	615
Terry Forster	16	614
Jerry Koosman	19	612
Willie Hernandez	10	604
Bob Friend	16	602
Al Worthington	14	602
Elias Sosa	12	601
Bobo Newsom	20	600
Ted Lyons	21	594
Mel Harder	20	582
Curt Simmons	20	569
Dolf Luque	20	550
Clark Griffith	20	416

Most Complete Games, Career

W ith the advent of the relief pitcher, pitching a complete ball game has become a rarity. But consider the fact that Cy Young started 818 games in his career, a major-league record. Young also holds the record for most career complete games, having finished an incredible 751 games. That means he completed over 90 percent of the games he started. No modern-day pitcher even comes close.

The names on the list look like a pitching roster in Cooperstown. Walter Johnson, Christy Mathewson, and Warren Spahn crack the top twenty.

Since today's managers are reluctant to burn out a pitcher's arm, it's a good bet that no contemporary pitcher will ever reach the top twenty. Many, like Steve Carlton and Ferguson Jenkins, have come close, but even they are almost 500 complete games behind Cy Young.

Gaylord Perry

RIGHT: *Walter Johnson*

MOST COMPLETE GAMES, CAREER

PITCHER	GAMES
Cy Young	751
Pud Galvin	641
Tim Keefe	554
Walter Johnson	531
Kid Nichols	531
Mickey Welch	525
John Clarkson	485
Old Hoss Radbourn	479
Tony Mullane	464
Jim McCormick	462
Gus Weyhing	448
Grover Alexander	436
Christy Mathewson	434
John Powell	422
Bill White	394
Amos Rusie	391
Vic Willis	387
Ed Plank	387
Warren Spahn	382
Jim Whitney	373
Bill Terry	368
Ted Lyons	356
Charlie Buffinton	350
Chick Fraser	342
George Mullin	339
Clark Griffith	337
Red Ruffing	335
Charles King	327
Al Orth	323
Fred Hutchinson	321
Burleigh Grimes	314
Joe McGinnity	314
Frank Donahue	312
Guy Hecker	310
Bill Dinneen	305
Robin Roberts	305
Gaylord Perry	303
Ted Breitenstein	300
Lefty Grove	300
Bob Caruthers	299
Emerson Hawley	297

Vern Kennedy	297
Ed Morris	297
Mark Baldwin	296
Tommy Bond	294
Wild Bill Donovan	290
Eppa Rixey	290
Early Wynn	290
Bob Mathews	289
Ellsworth Cunningham	286
Jack Stivetts	281
Wilbur Cooper	279
Bob Feller	279
Jack Taylor	278
John McMahon	277
Charles Getzein	277
Red Faber	275
John Dwyer	270
Jouett Meekin	270

Ferguson Jenkins	267
Jesse Tannehill	266
Elton Chamberlain	264
Matt Kilroy	264
Guy White	262
Jack Chesbro	261
Rube Waddell	261
Philip Ehret	260
Carl Hubbell	258
Larry Corcoran	256
Bob Gibson	255
Steve Carlton	254
Frank Killen	253
George Mercer	252
Paul Derringer	251
Sam Jones	250
Ed Walsh	250

ABOVE: *Ronald Reagan played Grover Cleveland Alexander in the 1952 film* The Winning Team.

Most Innings Pitched, Career

S ince the game began, it's always been three outs to an inning. And before any batter can swing, the pitcher must throw the ball. This list is comprised of the men who had the strength and endurance to continually hurl that ball toward the plate. Not surprisingly, the all-time record-holder is Cy Young. Basic mathematics will tell you that all but a few hundred of Young's innings were by way of his 751 complete games.

Others on the list could only hope for second place. The Number Two man, Pud Galvin, would have had to pitch another 158 complete games to overtake Young. Many on the list got there by mixing talent with a seemingly tireless arm. Don Sutton, Tom Seaver, and Phil Niekro got there by putting many successful years together.

MOST INNINGS PITCHED, CAREER

PITCHER	INNINGS
Cy Young	7377
Pud Galvin	5959
Walter Johnson	5923
Phil Niekro	5400⅔
Gaylord Perry	5352
Warren Spahn	5246
Grover Alexander	5188
Steve Carlton	5206⅔
Kid Nichols	5067
Tim Keefe	5043
Don Sutton	5002⅔
Mickey Welch	4784
Tom Seaver	4782
Christy Mathewson	4781
Robin Roberts	4689
Early Wynn	4560
Old Hoss Radbourn	4543
John Clarkson	4534
Jim Kaat	4527⅔
Tony Mullane	4506
Ferguson Jenkins	4498⅔
Eppa Rixey	4494
Tommy John	4467⅓
Jack Powell	4390
Red Ruffing	4335
Nolan Ryan	4327
Jim McCormick	4264
Bert Blyleven	4327
Ed Plank	4234
Burleigh Grimes	4178
Ted Lyons	4162
Red Faber	4087
Vic Willis	3994
Jim Palmer	3947⅓
Lefty Grove	3940
Bob Gibson	3885
Sam Jones	3884
Jerry Koosman	3839⅓
Bob Feller	3828
Waite Hoyt	3762
Jim Bunning	3759
Bobo Newsom	3758
Amos Rusie	3750
Paul Derringer	3646
Mickey Lolich	3640
Bob Friend	3612
Carl Hubbell	3591
Herb Pennock	3572
Earl Whitehill	3563
Bill White	3543
Bill Terry	3523
Juan Marichal	3506

BELOW: *Grover Cleveland Alexander*

RIGHT: *Walter Johnson*

Gaylord Perry

Steve Carlton

LEFT: The record number of innings pitched is 7,377, held by Cy Young. Pud Galvin, number 2 on the list, pitched only 5,959 innings.

Most Hits Allowed, Career

E verybody loves to hear the crack of the bat as the hitter makes contact. Everybody, that is, except the pitcher. For the pitcher, a hit is another step closer to yielding a run. And every run across the plate brings the pitcher closer to another notch in the loss column.

Most of the pitchers on this list made it to the Hall of Fame. For these memorable hurlers, yielding a hit only made them bear down harder to get the next batter out. The all-time leaders in this category, headed up by Cy Young, include Warren Spahn, Gaylord Perry, and Don Sutton.

For some of the real old-timers, the rules were really brutal. In 1887, bases on balls were counted as hits. So a batter, standing at the plate with the bat comfortably resting on his shoulders, could look at four pitched balls and get credited with a base hit!

Robin Roberts

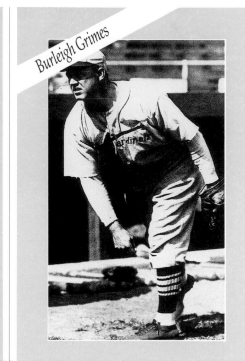

Burleigh Grimes

BELOW: *The durable Phil Niekro is approaching Pud Galvin's record for most hits allowed.*

LEFT: *Eppa Rixey*

MOST HITS ALLOWED, CAREER

PITCHER	HITS
Cy Young	7078
Pud Galvin	6334
Phil Niekro	5038
Gaylord Perry	4938
Walter Johnson	4920
Grover Alexander	4868
Kid Nichols	4854
Warren Spahn	4830
Gus Weyhing	4669
Steve Carlton	4652
Mickey Welch	4646
Eppa Rixey	4633
Jim Kaat	4620
Rob Roberts	4582
Tim Keefe	4524
Old Hoss Radbourn	4500
Ted Lyons	4489
Tommy John	4475
Burleigh Grimes	4406
Don Sutton	4402
John Clarkson	4376
John Powell	4323
Red Ruffing	4294
Early Wynn	4291
Tony Mullane	4238
Christy Mathewson	4203
Jim McCormick	4166
Ferguson Jenkins	4142
Red Faber	4104
Sam Jones	4084
Waite Hoyt	4037

A GALLERY
OF GREAT BASEBALL PLAYERS

The great baseball skills of Roberto Clemente and his leadership both on and off the field were ended in a tragic plane crash in 1972.

*A legend among legends
and listed in many batting
records, Mickey Mantle is
one of a handful of players
to hit four home runs in a
World Series.*

*Stan Musial demonstrates
the hitting stance that set
records for 22 years in the
big league.*

*José Canseco started his
major-league career with a
bang, hitting more than 30
home runs in his rookie
season.*

One of the best pinch-hitters around, Candy Maldonado consistently is near the top of the league in game-winning hits and run batted in.

TOP LEFT An excellent all-around ballplayer, Tony Gwynn hits, steals, and rarely makes an error in the outfield. He won his first Gold Glove in 1986.

TOP RIGHT The amazing Phil Niekro has been pitching his baffling knuckleball since 1964.

BOTTOM LEFT Pete Incaviglia is one of the handful of professional baseball players to make his major-league debut without serving in the minor leagues first.

BOTTOM RIGHT Ace reliever Goose Gossage is almost at the top of the career saves list — definitely Hall of Fame material.

Roger Maris, one of the greatest hitters in baseball history, broke Babe Ruth's single-season home-run record by hitting 61 dingers in 1961.

Powerful Don Baylor never
flinches from taking one
for the team. He has been
hit by a pitch more often
than any other player.

TOP LEFT Hard-hitting
Carlton Fisk is also a fine
defensive catcher. He is on
the list of players with the
most career home runs and
also on the list of catchers
with the fewest passed
balls in a season.

TOP RIGHT Joel Youngblood
holds one of baseball's
quirkier records — in 1982
he got a hit in a game
while playing as a Met,
was traded that day to
Montreal, and joined
Expos in time to suit up
and get a hit in that game
too.

BOTTOM LEFT Tony Armas is
in the illustrious company
of Babe Ruth and Roger
Maris on the list of players
with the most home runs
in a single season.

BOTTOM RIGHT The
powerful hitting of Wade
Boggs has been compared
to another great Red Sox
player — Ted Williams.

TOP LEFT Winner of the Cy Young award and the Rookie of the Year award, pitcher Roger Clemens has established a dominant position at a youthful age.

TOP RIGHT Baseball's strikeout king is the durable Nolan Ryan — no other pitcher even comes close to his strikeout total.

RIGHT A good defensive shortstop, Hubie Brooks is also an excellent hitter with a high slugging percentage.

RIGHT Veteran player Jim Rice began his career with the Boston Red Sox in 1974. It's hard to know whether his hitting or fielding is more important to the team.

ABOVE *Hard-hitting Dave Parker is well up on the list of players with the highest lifetime batting average.*

TOP LEFT *One of the very best outfielders is Dwight Evans. Patrolling the difficult right field of Fenway Park, Evans robs many a batter of a sure hit.*

TOP RIGHT *George Bell is one of baseball's best young hitters. In addition, he rarely walks and is very hard to strike out.*

BOTTOM LEFT *Gold Glove winner Jesse Barfield is one of the best right fielders ever to play the game. He's no slouch at the plate, either.*

BOTTOM RIGHT: *The great Reggie Jackson has been a big-leaguer for over 20 years – and setting hitting records for almost as long.*

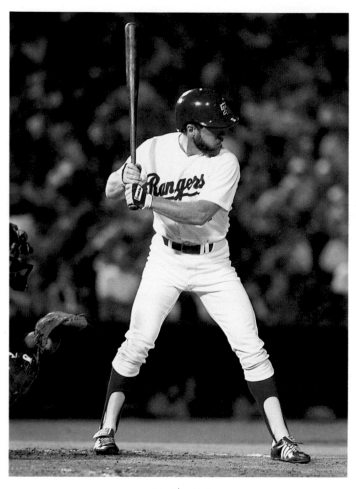

ABOVE: *Toby Harrah's long career has included long stints with the Texas Rangers and Cleveland Indians. A consistent hitter, his career average hovers at around .270.*

ABOVE Nolan Ryan has thrown more strikeouts than any other pitcher in baseball history.

TOP Catcher Johnny Bench, whose career spanned 17 years, was a key part of the famous Big Red Machine of the 1970s.

BOTTOM LEFT: *Powerful Don Baylor never flinches from taking one for the team. He has been hit by a pitch more often than any other player.*

BOTTOM RIGHT *Peter Rose played for the Cincinnati Reds from 1963 to 1978. In that time he led the league in hits six times. Rose ended his amazing career in 1984 with a lifetime total of 4,097 hits — the most in baseball history.*

ABOVE: *One of the finest all-round ball players active today, Dale Murphy occasionally is near the top of the league in batting state.*

RIGHT: *Called by some the purest hitter ever, Rod Carew here demonstrates the stance and concentration that helped him lead the league in hitting seven times in 18 years.*

ABOVE Roger Clemens has a good chance at adding another Cy Young Award to his collection.

Most Runs Allowed, Career

J ust as the great home-run hitters strike out every now and then, so do the game's phenomenal pitchers give up the occasional run. But just to be on this elite list means that some manager trusted a pitcher's prowess enough to allow a few runs to score.

A quick glance reveals the same names under the complete games and most-innings categories. With the contemporary usage of a relief staff, today's modern pitcher usually heads for the shower after giving up a few runs. So old-timers like Cy Young and Pud Galvin top the list. Nevertheless, a few venerable but still active hurlers, like Phil Niekro and Steve Carlton, have shown their worth enough times to stay in the game.

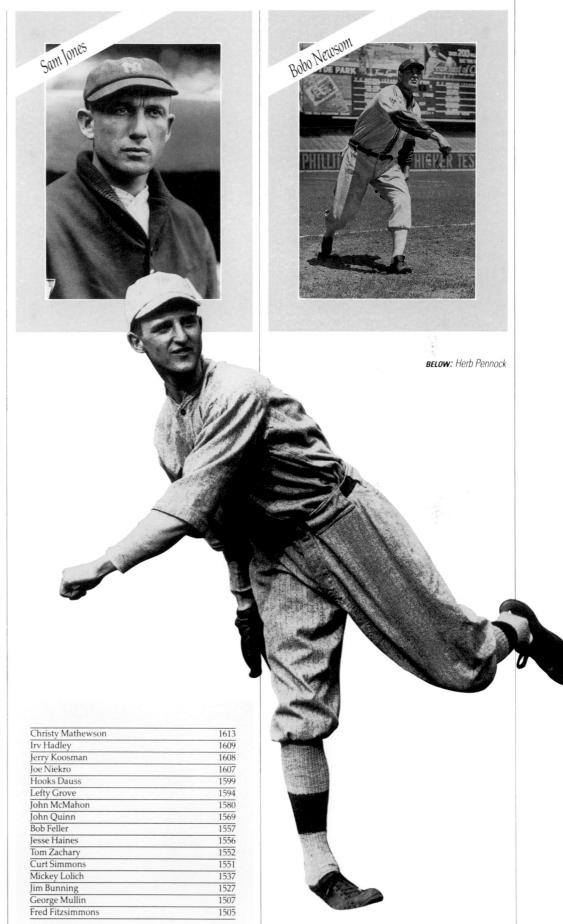

Sam Jones

Bobo Newsom

BELOW: Herb Pennock

MOST RUNS ALLOWED, CAREER

PITCHER	RUNS
Pud Galvin	3303
Cy Young	3168
Gus Weyhing	2770
Mickey Welch	2555
Tony Mullane	2520
Kid Nichols	2477
Tim Keefe	2461
John Clarkson	2396
Phil Niekro	2337
Old Hoss Radbourn	2300
Jim McCormick	2129
Gaylord Perry	2128
Red Ruffing	2117
Steve Carlton	2075
Jim Whitney	2060
Don Sutton	2060
Ted Lyons	2056
Burleigh Grimes	2048
Jim Kaat	2038
Early Wynn	2037
Earl Whitehill	2018
Warren Spahn	2016
Sam Jones	2008
Eppa Rixey	1986
Chick Fraser	1984
John Powell	1976
Robin Roberts	1962
Amos Rusie	1908
Bobo Newsom	1908
Walter Johnson	1902
Tommy John	1876
Ferguson Jenkins	1853
Grover Alexander	1851
Silver King	1834
Red Faber	1813
Jack Stivetts	1809
Waite Hoyt	1780
Nolan Ryan	1718
Mel Harder	1714
Al Orth	1711
Herb Pennock	1699
Tom Seaver	1674
Bert Blyleven	1664
Paul Derringer	1652
Bob Friend	1652
Vic Willis	1644
Frank Donahue	1640
George Uhle	1635
Christy Mathewson	1613
Irv Hadley	1609
Jerry Koosman	1608
Joe Niekro	1607
Hooks Dauss	1599
Lefty Grove	1594
John McMahon	1580
John Quinn	1569
Bob Feller	1557
Jesse Haines	1556
Tom Zachary	1552
Curt Simmons	1551
Mickey Lolich	1537
Jim Bunning	1527
George Mullin	1507
Fred Fitzsimmons	1505

Most Grand Slams Given Up, Career

T he bases are loaded. The crowd goes wild with anticipation as the batter steps up to the plate. Collectively, everyone is thinking grand slam. Everyone including the loneliest person in the ball park, the pitcher. On the mound, staring down the batter, the hurler concentrates, trying to avoid the ultimate pitching collapse. In many cases, the pitcher is one toss away from a trip to the locker room and the solitude of the showers.

Some of the members of this well-lathered list must have felt hexed. Three pitchers in particular, Ned Garver, Milt Pappas, and Jerry Reuss, were especially unlucky in bases-loaded situations. Leading the tally with nine each, these three spent many a game toweling off in the late innings.

Most of them were good hurlers who just had the knack of delivering a fat pitch with the bags loaded. Bert Blyleven, Mike Torrez, Ray Sadecki, and Early Wynn are just some members of the grand-slam club.

Bert Blyleven

Roy Face

BELOW: Bert Blyleven just makes it onto the list of most career grand slams given up.

MOST GRAND SLAMS GIVEN UP, CAREER

PITCHER	TOTAL
Ned Garver	9
Milt Pappas	9
Jerry Reuss	9
Jim Kaat	8
Lindy McDaniel	8
Roy Face	8
Bob Feller	8
Early Wynn	8
John Klippstein	8
Jim Brewer	8
Frank McGraw	8
Larry French	7
Jim Hearn	7
Jack Sanford	7
Lonnie Warneke	7
Ray Sadecki	7
Gaylord Perry	7
Mike Torrez	7
Bill Sherdel	7
Phil Niekro	7
Bert Blyleven	7

Most Strikeouts

I f you want to see how a strikeout pitcher can excite a crowd, just go to a game where Dwight Gooden is pitching for the New York Mets. They call him the Doctor because he's such an operator around the plate. With each mounting strikeout, the fans cheer louder as the letter "K" for strikeout is hung from the upper box seats.

But even Gooden has quite a way to go to make the list of the top strikeout artists in the game. Topping the list is Nolan Ryan, who has zapped 4,547 batters. In second place is Steve Carlton who, for years, battled Ryan for the strikeout lead.

Other "K" masters include Jim Bunning, Bob Gibson, and Gaylord Perry. To put Ryan's mark in perspective, realize that Dwight Gooden would have to strike out an average of 200 batters for over 21 seasons to near Ryan's figures!

Tom Seaver

BELOW: Bob Feller

MOST STRIKEOUTS

PITCHER	SO
Nolan Ryan	4547
Steve Carlton	4131
Tom Seaver	3640
Gaylord Perry	3534
Don Sutton	3530
Walter Johnson	3508
Phil Niekro	3342
Bert Blyleven	3286
Ferguson Jenkins	3192
Bob Gibson	3117
Jim Bunning	2855
Mickey Lolich	2832
Cy Young	2819
Warren Spahn	2583
Jerry Koosman	2556
Bob Feller	2581
Tim Keefe	2538
Christy Mathewson	2505
Don Drysdale	2486
Jim Kaat	2461
Sam McDowell	2453
Luis Tiant	2416
Sandy Koufax	2396
Robin Roberts	2357
Early Wynn	2334
George Waddell	2310
Juan Marichal	2303
Lefty Grove	2266
Jim Palmer	2212
Grover Alexander	2198
Vida Blue	2175
Camilo Pascual	2167
Tommy John	2146
Ed Plank	2112
Bobo Newsom	2082
Dazzy Vance	2045
Catfish Hunter	2012

Most Bases on Balls Allowed, Career

S ome pitchers just fire the ball toward the plate, concentrating more on speed than placement. Others, however, have established themselves as experts in "hitting the corner" for strikes. The list of those pitchers who walked the most batters includes some of the top hurlers in baseball history.

Nolan Ryan, considered one of the hardest throwers in the game, has walked a record 2,268 batters. Ryan is a master at pitch location. When he can't blow a batter away with speed, Ryan relies on getting close strikes. The umpires don't always see it his way. Maybe the umpire, like the batter, has trouble watching the speeding baseball.

As in some other categories, longevity plays a part here. For a pitcher to accumulate enough walks to make this list, it helps if his career is extended. That too requires a special talent – being good enough to stay in the starting rotation despite giving up all those bases on balls.

MOST BASES ON BALLS ALLOWED, CAREER

PITCHER	BB
Nolan Ryan	2355
Steve Carlton	1828
Phil Niekro	1803
Early Wynn	1775
Bob Feller	1764
Bobo Newson	1732
Amos Rusie	1637
Gus Weyhing	1569
Red Ruffing	1541
Irv Hadley	1442
Warren Spahn	1434
Earl Whitehill	1431
Sam Jones	1396
Tom Seaver	1390
Tony Mullane	1379
Gaylord Perry	1379
Mike Torrez	1371
Walter Johnson	1353
Bob Gibson	1336
Chick Fraser	1332
Don Sutton	1313
Sam McDowell	1312
Jim Palmer	1311
Mickey Welch	1305
Burleigh Grimes	1295
Mark Baldwin	1285
Allie Reynolds	1261
Les Bush	1260
Bob Lemon	1251
Hal Newhouser	1249
Kid Nichols	1245
Bill Terry	1244
Tim Keefe	1225
Red Faber	1213
Cy Young	1209

Tom Seaver

Early Wynn

ABOVE: *With 1,775 career walks allowed, Early Wynn is near the top of the list.*

Lowest Career ERA, 3,000 or More Innings

U nlike some statistics, such as most innings pitched or wins, this category equalizes the different eras of the game. The list of those with the lowest earned run average includes old-timers like Walter Johnson and Grover Cleveland Alexander as well as "newcomers" like Tom Seaver and Jim Palmer.

A statistics purist might argue that the modern trend toward relief pitchers detrimentally affects the starter's ERA. For example, if a relief pitcher enters the game with the bases loaded and serves up a home-run ball, he's only charged with one of the earned runs. The starting pitcher, however, headed toward the showers gets the additional three runs tacked on to his total, thus inflating his ERA.

In any event, a pitcher's aim is to prevent the other team from scoring. All the hurlers on this list were quite adept in reaching their goal. Don Drysdale, Juan Marichal, and Carl Hubbell ended their careers by joining a few others with sub-3.00 earned run averages.

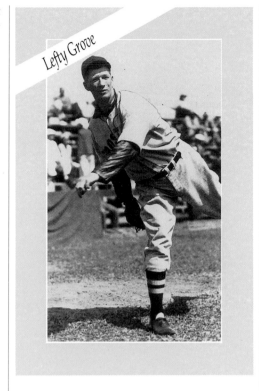

Lefty Grove

Don Drysdale

RIGHT: Jim Bunning

LOWEST CAREER ERA, 3,000 OR MORE INNINGS

PITCHER	IP	ERA
Walter Johnson	4195	2.37
Grover Alexander	4822	2.56
Whitey Ford	3171	2.74
Tom Seaver	4782	2.86
Jim Palmer	3947⅓	2.86
Stan Coveleski	3071	2.88
Juan Marichal	3506	2.89
Wilbur Cooper	3482	2.89
Bob Gibson	3885	2.91
Carl Mays	3022	2.92
Don Drysdale	3432	2.95
Carl Hubbell	3591	2.98
Lefty Grove	3940	3.06
Warren Spahn	5246	3.08
Bert Blyleven	3988	3.08
Gaylord Perry	5352	3.10
Steve Carlton	5054⅔	3.11
Nolan Ryan	4115⅓	3.15
Eppa Rixey	4494	3.15
Red Faber	4087	3.15
Don Sutton	5002⅔	3.20
Tommy John	4279⅔	3.23
Dolf Luque	3221	3.24
Bob Feller	3828	3.25
Dutch Leonard	3220	3.25
Catfish Hunter	3449	3.26
Vida Blue	3344	3.26
Jim Bunning	3759	3.27
Bill Pierce	3305	3.27
Phil Niekro	5265	3.27
Luis Tiant	3485⅔	3.30
Bucky Walters	3104	3.30
Claude Osteen	3459	3.30
George Dauss	3374	3.32
Ferguson Jenkins	4498⅔	3.34
Jerry Koosman	3839⅓	3.36
Lee Meadows	3151	3.38
Rob Roberts	4689	3.40
Larry Jackson	3262	3.40
Milt Pappas	3186	3.40
Mickey Lolich	3640	3.44
Larry French	3152	3.44
Jim Perry	3287	3.44
Jim Kaat	4527⅓	3.46
Paul Derringer	3646	3.46
Les Bush	3088	3.49
Jerry Reuss	3218⅔	3.50
Joe Niekro	3426	3.50

Most Career Victories

E very kid who has ever set foot on the pitching mound dreams of tossing his team to victory. Fortunately for the pitchers on this list the dream very often came true. In this distinguished crowd, Cy Young was the only pitcher to win over 500 games. Considered by many the greatest pitcher of all time, Young won an outstanding 511 games during his major-league career.

The members on the most-victories list include some current and future Hall of Famers. The old-timers include Walter Johnson, Christy Mathewson, and Grover Alexander. Some of the more contemporary pitchers, like Warren Spahn, Gaylord Perry, and Tom Seaver, quickly established themselves as superstars.

Among the contenders still active, Phil Niekro and Don Sutton continue to increase their victory totals season after season.

Chief Bender

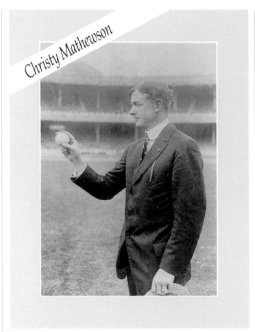

Christy Mathewson

BELOW: With 511 career victories, Cy Young is the winningest pitcher in baseball history.

MOST CAREER VICTORIES

PITCHER	W	L	Pct.
Cy Young	511	313	.620
Walter Johnson	416	279	.599
Christy Mathewson	373	188	.665
Grover Alexander	373	208	.642
Warren Spahn	363	245	.597
Kid Nichols	361	208	.634
Pud Galvin	361	309	.539
Tim Keefe	342	224	.604
John Clarkson	327	176	.650
Steve Carlton	329	243	.575
Don Sutton	321	250	.562
Phil Niekro	318	274	.537
Gaylord Perry	314	265	.542
Tom Seaver	311	205	.603
Old Hoss Radbourn	308	191	.617
Mickey Welch	307	209	.595
Ed Plank	305	181	.628
Lefty Grove	300	141	.680
Early Wynn	300	244	.551
Robin Roberts	286	245	.539
Tony Mullane	285	213	.572
Ferguson Jenkins	284	226	.557
Jim Kaat	283	237	.544
Tommy John	277	216	.562
Red Ruffing	273	225	.548
Burleigh Grimes	270	212	.560
Jim Palmer	268	152	.638
Bob Feller	266	162	.621
Eppa Rixey	266	251	.515
Jim McCormick	265	215	.552
Gus Weyhing	262	224	.539
Nolan Ryan	261	242	.534
Ted Lyons	260	230	.531
Red Faber	254	212	.545
Carl Hubbell	253	154	.622
Bob Gibson	251	174	.591
Joe McGinnity	247	145	.630
John Powell	247	254	.493
Vic Willis	244	204	.545
Bert Blyleven	244	209	.538
Juan Marichal	243	142	.631

LEFT: Three-Finger Brown

Walter Johnson

Amos Rusie	241	158	.604
Clark Griffith	240	140	.632
Herb Pennock	240	162	.597
Waite Hoyt	237	182	.566
Whitey Ford	236	106	.690
Charlie Buffinton	230	151	.604
Luis Tiant	229	172	.571
Sam Jones	229	217	.513
Will White	227	167	.576
Catfish Hunter	224	166	.574
Jim Bunning	224	184	.549
Mel Harder	223	186	.545
Paul Derringer	223	212	.513
George Dauss	222	182	.550
Jerry Koosman	222	209	.515
Joe Niekro	220	203	.520
Earl Whitehill	218	186	.540
Bob Caruthers	217	101	.682
Fred Fitzsimmons	217	146	.598
Mickey Lolich	217	191	.532
Wilbur Cooper	216	178	.548
Stan Coveleski	215	141	.604
Jim Perry	215	174	.553
John Quinn	212	181	.539
George Mullin	212	181	.539
Bill Pierce	211	169	.555
Bobo Newsom	211	222	.487
Ed Cicotte	210	149	.585
Jesse Haines	210	158	.571
Vida Blue	209	161	.565
Milt Pappas	209	164	.560
Don Drysdale	209	166	.557
3-Finger Brown	208	111	.652
Chief Bender	208	112	.650
Carl Mays	208	126	.623
Bob Lemon	207	128	.618
Hal Newhouser	207	150	.580
Silver King	206	152	.575
Jack Stivetts	205	128	.616
Bill Terry	205	197	.510
Lew Burdette	203	144	.585
Charlie Root	201	160	.557
Rube Marquard	201	177	.532
George Uhle	200	166	.546

The 20 Victories Club

Like hitting .333 or pounding out 40 homers, pitching 20 victories in a season is the understood mark of a good year. Since more often than not today a relief pitcher finishes the game, starters are sometimes deprived of the chance to get the win, especially when their team rallies.

But regardless of the era, hurling a 20-win season has always meant success. Sitting atop the list is Cy Young, who set the record with 16 seasons of 20 or more wins. Finishing tied for second place are Christy Mathewson and Warren Spahn, who each won 20 for 13 years.

Even some of the greatest pitchers of only a few years ago, like Juan Marichal and Bob Lemon, couldn't approach the old-timers. One factor is that pitchers like Young and Mathewson, playing on starting rotations of only three or four pitchers, got the ball more often.

THE 20 VICTORIES CLUB

PITCHER	YEARS
Cy Young	16
Christy Mathewson	13
Warren Spahn	13
Walter Johnson	12
Kid Nichols	11
Jim Galvin	10
Grover Alexander	9
Old Hoss Radbourn	9
Mickey Welch	9
John Clarkson	8
Lefty Grove	8
Jim McCormick	8
Joe McGinnity	8
Tony Mullane	8
Amos Rusie	8
Jim Palmer	8
Charlie Buffinton	7
Clark Griffith	7
Tim Keefe	7
Bob Lemon	7
Ed Plank	7
Gus Weyhing	7
Vic Willis	7
Ferguson Jenkins	7
Mordecai Brown	6
Bob Caruthers	6
Bob Feller	6
Wes Ferrell	6
Juan Marichal	6
Robin Roberts	6
Jesse Tannehill	6
Steve Carlton	6
Tommy Bond	5
Jack Chesbro	5
Larry Corcoran	5
Stan Coveleski	5
Bob Gibson	5
Burleigh Grimes	5
Carl Hubbell	5
Charles King	5
John McMahon	5
Carl Mays	5
George Mullin	5
Deacon Phillippe	5
Jack Stivetts	5
Hippo Vaughn	5
Jo Jo White	5
Jim Whitney	5
Early Wynn	5
Catfish Hunter	5
Tom Seaver	5
Gaylord Perry	5

Christy Mathewson, *BELOW LEFT*, is second on the list with 20 victories in a season 13 times, whilst Cy Young, *BOTTOM LEFT*, pitched his team to 20 victories for 16 seasons.

BELOW: Warren Spahn is tied with Mathewson for second place on the list.

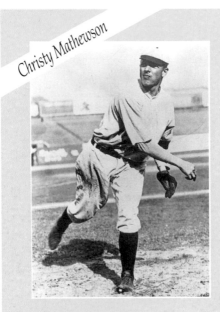

Christy Mathewson

Cy Young

Most Career Shutouts

According to many of the game's experts, good pitching beats good hitting. These successful pitchers were so good that they often shut out their opponents. Walter Johnson leads the bunch with 110 career shutouts. Others who had some good days were Cy Young, Warren Spahn, and Tom Seaver.

Then, of course, there were fastball merchants like Bob Gibson, Don Drysdale, and Sandy Kuofax, who at times made hitters look just plain silly at the plate.

When they were hot, the members of this special list were unbeatable. Hand them the ball and after a neat, clean nine innings, it was time for the victory celebration.

MOST CAREER SHUTOUTS

PITCHER	GAMES
Walter Johnson	110
Grover Alexander	90
Christy Mathewson	83
Cy Young	77
Ed Plank	64
Warren Spahn	63
Tom Seaver	61
Ed Walsh	58
Don Sutton	58
Pud Galvin	57
Bob Gibson	56
Steve Carlton	55
Nolan Ryan	54
Bert Blyleven	54
Jim Palmer	53
Gaylord Perry	53
Juan Marichal	52
Mordecai Brown	50
George Waddell	50
Vic Willis	50
Early Wynn	49
Don Drysdale	49
Luis Tiant	49
Ferguson Jenkins	49
Kid Nichols	48
Jack Powell	46
Doc White	46
Babe Adams	45
Addie Joss	45
Red Ruffing	45
Rob Roberts	45
Whitey Ford	45
Tommy John	45
Phil Niekro	45
Bob Feller	44
Milt Pappas	43
Bucky Walters	42
Catfish Hunter	42
Chief Bender	41
Mickey Lolich	41
Hippo Vaughn	41
Mickey Welch	41
Larry French	40
Sandy Koufax	40
Jim Bunning	40
Mel Stottlemyre	40
Claude Osteen	40
Tim Keefe	40

Three-Finger Brown

Don Drysdale

BELOW: With 110 shutouts, Walter Johnson leads the list by 20 games.

Most Complete-Game 1–0 Victories

A ll pitchers want their teams to put a few runs on the scoreboard. The more runs a pitcher has behind him, the less pressure there is on the mound. But for some hurlers, one run was often enough.

Locked in these close pitching duels, the players here were able to find a little something extra on the fastball or put a little more spin on the curve.

Leading the list of the too-close-for-comfort club is Walter Johnson with 38 1–0 games under his belt. Others, like Bert Blyleven and Steve Carlton, seem to thrive under the strain of close games.

Winning these 1–0 games is the mark of a true competitor. It's only natural that most of these success stories are enshrined in the Hall of Fame.

LEFT: Ed Plank

RIGHT: Sandy Koufax hams it up for the camera after pitching his 100th National League victory in 1964.

MOST COMPLETE-GAME 1–0 VICTORIES

PITCHER	GAMES
Walter Johnson	38
Grover Alexander	17
Christy Mathewson	14
Bert Blyleven	14
Ed Plank	13
Ed Walsh	13
Doc White	13
Cy Young	13
Dean Chance	13
Stan Coveleski	12
Gaylord Perry	12
Steve Carlton	12
George Rucker	11
Charlie Nichols	11
Ferguson Jenkins	11
Joe Bush	10
Paul Derringer	10
Bill Doak	10
Addie Joss	10
Dick Rudolph	10
Hippo Vaughn	10
Lefty Tyler	10
Warren Spahn	10
Sandy Koufax	10
Nolan Ryan	10

Perfect Games

T he optimum performance for a pitcher is to toss a perfect game. For 27 consecutive outs no batter reaches first base. Since 1900, only 11 pitchers have thrown perfect games. Once the game gets into the seventh or eighth inning, even those fans on the losing side start cheering to see a piece of baseball history.

The most memorable perfect game was thrown by Don Larsen of the New York Yankees. On October 8, 1956, Larsen pitched the only perfect game in World Series history against the Brooklyn Dodgers.

In 1959, Harvey Haddix of the Pirates became the only pitcher to throw a perfect game, yet lose! Haddix pitched 12 perfect innings before a throwing error led to an eventual Milwaukee score. The Pirates lost the game, 1–0.

The last perfect game was pitched by Mike Witt of the California Angels on September 30, 1984. Witt shutdown the Texas Rangers by a score of 1–0.

BELOW: *A perfect game is very rare. Only one man has ever pitched a perfect game in a World Series – Don Larsen in 1956.*

RIGHT: *Babe Ruth (left) and Ernie Shore.*

PERFECT GAMES

DATE	PITCHER	TEAMS	SCORE
12 June 1904	Cy Young	Boston v. Philadelphia	3–0
2 Oct 1908	Addie Joss	Cleveland v. Chicago	1–0
23 June 1917	Ernie Shore	Boston v. Washington	4–0
30 April 1922	Charlie Robertson	Chicago v. Detroit	2–0
8 Oct 1956	Don Larsen	New York v. Brooklyn (World Series)	2–0
26 May 1959	Harvey Haddix	Pittsburgh v. Milwaukee	0–1
21 June 1964	Jim Bunning	Philadelphia v. New York	6–0
9 Sept 1965	Sandy Koufax	Los Angeles v. Chicago	1–0
8 May 1968	Catfish Hunter	Oakland v. Minnesota	4–0
15 May 1981	Len Barker	Cleveland v. Toronto	3–0
30 Sept 1984	Mike Witt	California v. Texas	1–0

Harvey Haddix

Sandy Koufax

Pitchers with at Least 12 Straight Victories in a Season

S ometimes a ballplayer gets hot and puts together a string of well-played games. Usually these occur for offensive positions, where the player gets a chance to extend a streak every day. For pitchers, who generally get into a game only every four or five days, the chance to run a long streak of good fortune is rare.

A few pitchers have been able to win at least 12 straight victories in one season. To accomplish this feat, good pitching and good luck must stay with the hurler for almost two months.

The post-1900 record is held by Rube Marquard of the 1912 New York Giants. Marquard put together a string of 19 straight wins. More recently, Gaylord Perry won 15 straight for the 1974 Cleveland Indians. Dwight Gooden of the New York Mets took away 15 straight during his phenomenal 1985 season. Roger Clemens helped his Cy Young Award effort by winning 14 straight games in 1986.

RIGHT: Burt Hooten

Rick Sutcliffe

BELOW: Phil Regan

PITCHERS WITH AT LEAST 12 STRAIGHT VICTORIES IN A SEASON

NATIONAL LEAGUE

YEAR	PITCHER	WON
1888	Tim Keefe, New York	19
1912	Rube Marquard, New York	19
1884	Old Hoss Radbourn, Providence	18
1885	Mickey Welch, New York	17
1890	John Luby, Chicago	17
1959	Roy Face, Pittsburgh	17
1886	Jim McCormick, Chicago	16
1936	Carl Hubbell, New York	16
1947	Ewell Blackwell, Cincinnati	16
1962	John Sanford, San Francisco	16
1924	Dazzy Vance, Brooklyn	15
1968	Bob Gibson, St. Louis	15
1972	Steve Carlton, Philadelphia	15
1885	Jim McCormick, Chicago	14
1886	Jocko Flynn, Chicago	14
1904	Joe McGinnity, New York	14
1909	Ed Reulbach, Chicago	14
1984	Rick Sutcliffe, Chicago	14
1985	Dwight Gooden, New York	14
1880	Larry Corcoran, Chicago	13
1884	Charles Buffinton, Boston	13
1892	Cy Young, Cleveland	13
1896	Frank Dwyer, Cincinnati	13
1909	Christy Mathewson, New York	13
1910	Deacon Phillippe, Pittsburgh	13
1927	Burleigh Grimes, New York	13
1956	Brooks Lawrence, Cincinatti	13
1966	Phil Regan, Los Angeles	13
1971	Dock Ellis, Pittsburgh	13
1885	John Clarkson, Chicago	13
1886	Charlie Ferguson, Philadelphia	12
1902	John Chesbro, Pittsburgh	12
1904	Hooks Wiltse, New York	12
1906	Ed Reulbach, Chicago	12
1914	Dick Rudolph, Boston	12
1975	Burt Hooton, Los Angeles	12

AMERICAN LEAGUE

YEAR	PITCHER	WON
1912	Walter Johnson, Washington	16
1912	Joe Wood, Boston	16
1931	Lefty Grove, Philadelphia	16
1934	Schoolboy Rowe, Detroit	16
1932	General Crowder, Washington	15
1937	John Allen, Cleveland	15
1969	Dave McNally, Baltimore	15
1974	Gaylord Perry, Cleveland	15
1904	Jack Chesbro, New York	14
1913	Walter Johnson, Washington	14
1914	Chief Bender, Philadelphia	14
1928	Lefty Grove, Philadelphia	14
1961	Whitey Ford, New York	14
1980	Steve Stone, Baltimore	14
1986	Roger Clemens, Boston	14
1924	Walter Johnson, Washington	13
1925	Stan Coveleski, Washington	13
1930	Wes Ferrell, Cleveland	13
1940	Bobo Newsom, Detroit	13
1949	Ellis Kinder, Boston	13
1971	Dave McNally, Baltimore	13
1973	Catfish Hunter, Oakland	13
1978	Ron Guidry, New York	13
1983	LaMarr Hoyt, Chicago	13
1985	Ron Guidry, New York	13
1901	Cy Young, Boston	12
1910	Russ Ford, New York	12
1914	Hubert Leonard, Boston	12
1929	Tom Zachary, New York	12
1931	George Earnshaw, Philadelphia	12
1938	Johnny Allen, Cleveland	12
1939	Atley Donald, New York	12
1946	Boo Ferriss, Boston	12
1961	Luis Arroyo, New York	12
1963	Whitey Ford, New York	12
1968	Dave McNally, Baltimore	12
1971	Pat Dobson, Baltimore	12

Pitchers with at Least 12 Straight Losses in a Season

For some pitchers, it didn't pay even to get out of bed – not just for a day, but for weeks. When a pitcher is in a slump, he might lose three or four games in a row. Then the hits stop falling, his infield makes the double play, and soon he's back in the win column. But for some unlucky hurlers, the losses kept piling up.

In the early days of the New York Mets, the losses were more common than wins. To sum up their futile 1962 season, one can point to Roger Craig's 18 straight losses and his teammate Craig Anderson's 16 straight defeats. Just so they didn't feel totally devastated, Bob Miller joined the Mets in 1962 only to drop 12 straight.

The old saying that what goes up must come down certainly applies to Rube Marquard. After winning 19 straight in 1912, Marquard dropped 12 in a row in 1914.

YEAR	PITCHER	LOST
1930	Dutch Henry, Chicago	13
1943	Lum Harris, Philadelphia	13
1982	Terry Felton, Minnesota	13
1929	Red Ruffing, Boston	12

YEAR	PITCHER	LOST
1940	Walt Masterson, Washington	12
1945	Bobo Newsom, Philadelphia	12
1945	Steve Gerkin, Philadelphia	12
1953	Charlie Bishop, Philadelphia	12

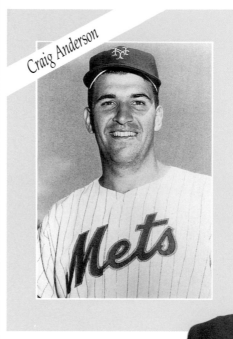

Craig Anderson

Mike Parrott

PITCHERS WITH AT LEAST 12 STRAIGHT LOSSES IN A SEASON

NATIONAL LEAGUE

YEAR	PITCHER	LOST
1910	Cliff Curtis, Boston	18
1963	Roger Craig, New York	18
1876	Dory Dean, Cincinatti	16
1899	Jim Hughey, Cleveland	16
1962	Craig Anderson, New York	16
1887	Frank Gilmore, Washington	14
1899	Fred Bates, Cleveland	14
1908	Jim Pastorius, Brooklyn	14
1911	Buster Brown, Boston	14
1884	Sam Moffatt, Cleveland	13
1917	Burleigh Grimes, Pittsburgh	13
1922	Joe Oeschger, Boston	13
1935	Ben Cantwell, Boston	13
1948	Dutch McCall, Chicago	13
1880	Blondie Purcell, Cincinatti	12
1883	John Coleman, Philadelphia	12
1902	Henry Thielman, Cincinatti	12
1905	Mal Eason, Brooklyn	12
1914	Rube Marquard, New York	12
1914	Pete Schneider, Cincinatti	12
1928	Russ Miller, Philadelphia	12
1933	Si Johnson, Cincinatti	12
1939	Max Butcher, Phil.–Pitts.	12
1940	Hugh Mulcahy, Philadelphia	12
1962	Bob Miller, New York	12
1972	Ken Reynolds, Philadelphia	12

AMERICAN LEAGUE

YEAR	PITCHER	LOST
1909	Bob Groom, Washington	19
1916	Jack Nabors, Philadelphia	19
1980	Mike Parrott, Seattle	16
1906	Joe Harris, Boston	14
1949	Howie Judson, Chicago	14
1949	Paul Calvert, Washington	14
1979	Matt Keough, Oakland	14
1914	Guy Morton, Cleveland	13
1920	Roy Moore, Philadelphia	13

LEFT: Bob Miller

30 Victories at Least Twice

The last pitcher to win 30 games in one year was Denny McClain of the 1968 Detroit Tigers – he won 31. Winning 30 games today, with each club carrying four or five pitchers, seems like an impossible task, but there was a time when it was more common.

These pitchers won 30 or more games at least twice in their career. Surprisingly, Cy Young is not on top of the list. Young won 30 or more only five times in his career.

The leader of the list is Kid Nichols, who won 30 or more an incredible seven times. That means that Nichols, who won a total of 361 times, had more victories in just those seven years than Hall of Famer Don Drysdale had in his entire career!

BELOW: *Grover Cleveland Alexander managed to get 30 wins in a season only three times.*

Kid Nichols

30 VICTORIES AT LEAST TWICE

PITCHER	YEARS
Kid Nichols	7
John Clarkson	6
Tim Keefe	6
Tony Mullane	5
Cy Young	5
Tommy Bond	4
Larry Corcoran	4
Jim McCormick	4
Christy Mathewson	4
Charles King	4
Will White	4
Mickey Welch	4
Pud Galvin	3
Fred Hutchison	3
Bob Caruthers	3
Bob Mathews	3
Grover Alexander	3
Ed Morris	3
Old Hoss Radbourn	3
Amos Rusie	3
George Haddock	2
Walter Johnson	2
Guy Hecker	2
Dave Foutz	2
Frank Killen	2
Joe McGinnity	2
John McMahon	2
Monte Ward	2
Jack Stivetts	2
Tom Ramsey	2
Gus Weyhing	2
Jim Whitney	2

Most Career Wins by a Relief Pitcher

M ost career wins by a relief pitcher is a difficult category to analyze. Since the primary job of the "stopper" in the bullpen is to save a game, a relief pitcher credited with a win, in most cases, gave up the go-ahead run. Then the manager decided to leave him in and his team rallied to win the game.

To qualify for this list, a reliever must have tossed quite a few games and at least kept the opposition within striking distance. The all-time leader in the category is Hoyt Wilhelm, with 123 career wins. Following closely are Lindy McDaniel with 119 and Rollie Fingers who piled up 107 career wins.

Among the active bullpen stoppers Goose Gossage, Gene Garber, and Kent Tekulve are approaching the century mark.

Kent Tekulve

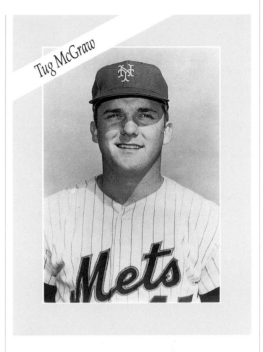

Tug McGraw

LEFT: Famed reliever Goose Gossage is sixth on the career wins list – and climbing.

MOST CAREER WINS BY A RELIEF PITCHER

RELIEVER	WINS
Hoyt Wilhelm	123
Lindy McDaniel	119
Rollie Fingers	107
Sparky Lyle	99
Roy Face	96
Goose Gossage	92
Mike Marshall	92
Don McMahon	90
Tug McGraw	89
Clay Carroll	88
Gene Garber	86
Kent Tekulve	85
Bill Campbell	80
Stu Miller	79
Ron Perranoski	79
Tom Burgmeier	79
Gary Lavelle	78
Bob Stanley	73
Johnny Murphy	73
John Hiller	72
Dick Hall	71
Pedro Borbon	69
Bruce Sutter	67
Al Hrabosky	64
Clem Labine	63
Darold Knowles	63
Mark Clear	62
Dick Farrell	62
Frank Linzy	62
Jim Brewer	62
Grant Jackson	62
Dave LaRoche	62

Most Saves Sinces 1969

The new knight in shining armor of the baseball world is the relief pitcher. Summoned from the bullpen, the relief pitcher takes the mound to save his team from disaster. Some are more successful than others.

These chosen few, the team stoppers, are utilized in late-inning situations, often with the game on the line. Rollie Fingers, famous for his handlebar mustache, is the all-time leader with 341 saves. Many of the toppers of the stoppers are still active. Goose Gossage, Dan Quisenberry, and Kent Tekulve still are called upon to save the game and the day.

Others, like Dave Righetti, a converted starter for the New York Yankees, established their relief expertise quickly and are destined to zoom up the list.

MOST SAVES SINCE 1969

PITCHER	SAVES
Rollie Fingers	341
Goose Gossage	289
Bruce Sutter	286
Sparky Lyle	238
Dan Quisenberry	237
Hoyt Wilhelm	227
Gene Garber	212
Roy Face	193
Jeff Reardon	193
Mike Marshall	188
Tug McGraw	180

Lee Smith	180
Ron Perranoski	179
Kent Tekulve	179
Lindy McDaniel	172
Stu Miller	154
Don McMahon	153
Ted Abernathy	148
Dave Giusti	145
Clay Carroll	143
Darold Knowles	143
Dave Righetti	138
Gary Lavelle	136
Greg Minton	134
Jim Brewer	132

Lee Smith

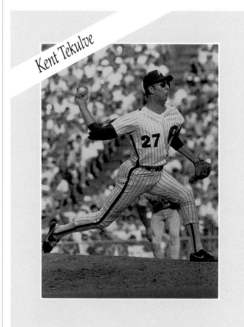

Kent Tekulve

Dan Quisenberry fires off a pitch using his feared submarine delivery.

Jeff Reardon

Most Saves, Year by Year

S ince the official save record began being kept in 1969, a number of relievers have distinguished themselves by besting the other stoppers in their respective league. In 1987, two newcomers cracked the list. In the American League, Toronto's Tom Henke topped Jeff Reardon and Dave Righetti with a league-leading 34 saves. Over in the National League, Philadelphia's Steve Bedrosian saved 40 games.

Although six shy of Dave Righetti's all-time record of 46 saves, Bedrosian's mark is truly incredible when you consider that the 1987 Phillies only won 80 games!

A few players, such as Mike Marshall and Rollie Fingers, were able to win the honors in both the American and National Leagues.

Todd Warrell

Lee Smith

RIGHT: *Steve Bodrosian saved 40 games in 1987 to lead the National League.*

MOST SAVES, YEAR BY YEAR

AMERICAN LEAGUE

YEAR	RELIEVER	TEAM	SAVES
1969	Ron Perranoski	Minnesota	31
1970	Ron Perranoski	Minnesota	34
1971	Ken Sanders	Milwaukee	31
1972	Sparky Lyle	New York	35
1973	John Hiller	Detroit	38
1974	Terry Forster	Chicago	24
1975	Goose Gossage	New York	26
1976	Sparky Lyle	New York	23
1977	Bill Campbell	Boston	31
1978	Goose Gossage	New York	27
1979	Mike Marshall	Minnesota	32
1980	Dan Quisenberry	Kansas City	33
1980	Goose Gossage	New York	33
1981	Rollie Fingers	Milwaukee	28
1982	Dan Quisenberry	Kansas City	35
1983	Dan Quisenberry	Kansas City	45
1984	Dan Quisenberry	Kansas City	44
1985	Dan Quisenberry	Kansas City	37
1986	Dave Righetti	New York	37
1987	Tom Henke	Toronto	34

NATIONAL LEAGUE

YEAR	RELIEVER	TEAM	SAVES
1969	Fred Gladding	Houston	29
1970	Wayne Granger	Cincinnati	35
1971	Dave Giusti	Pittsburgh	30
1972	Clay Carroll	Cincinnati	37
1973	Mike Marshall	Montreal	31
1974	Mike Marshall	Los Angeles	21
1975	Al Hrabosky	St. Louis	22
1975	Rawley Eastwick	Cincinnati	22
1976	Rawley Eastwick	Cincinnati	26
1977	Rollie Fingers	San Diego	35
1978	Rollie Fingers	San Diego	37
1979	Bruce Sutter	Chicago	37
1980	Bruce Sutter	Chicago	28
1981	Bruce Sutter	St. Louis	25
1982	Bruce Sutter	St. Louis	36
1983	Lee Smith	Chicago	29
1984	Bruce Sutter	St. Louis	45
1985	Jeff Reardon	Montreal	41
1986	Todd Worrell	St. Louis	36
1987	Steve Bedrosian	Philadelphia	40

Single-Season Save Records, by Team

W hen the game is on the line and the other team starts filling up the bases, the manager strides to the mound and motions toward the bullpen. In a matter of minutes, the ace stopper of the staff is ready to stop the rally.

Every team usually has one main stopper, although certain teams are fortunate enough to have two, like Jesse Orosco and Roger McDowell of the 1986 Mets. But for the most part only one man is summoned to get those crucial final outs – the bullpen ace.

The list of team single-season save records includes some of the game's most formidable closers. Included are such stoppers as Yankee hurler Dave Righetti, Toronto star Tom Henke, Steve "Bedrock" Bedrosian of the Philadelphia Phillies, and Dave Smith of the Houston Astros.

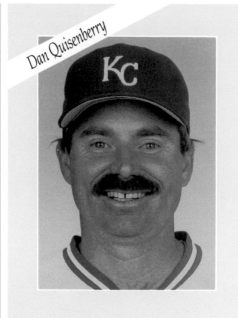
Dan Quisenberry

Gene Garber

LEFT: Kent Tekulve

SINGLE-SEASON SAVE RECORDS, BY TEAM

AMERICAN LEAGUE

TEAM	RELIEVER	YEAR	SAVES
Baltimore	Don Aase	1986	34
Boston	Bob Stanley	1983	33
California	Donnie Moore	1985	31
Chicago	Bob James	1985	32
Cleveland	Ernie Camacho	1984	23
Detroit	John Hiller	1977	38
Kansas City	Dan Quisenberry	1983	45
Milwaukee	Ken Sanders	1971	31
Minnesota	Ron Perranoski	1970	34
New York	Dave Righetti	1986	46
Oakland	Bill Caudill	1984	36
Seattle	Bill Caudill	1983	26
Texas	Jim Kern	1979	29
Toronto	Tom Henke	1986	27

NATIONAL LEAGUE

TEAM	RELIEVER	YEAR	SAVES
Atlanta	Gene Garber	1982	30
Chicago	Bruce Sutter	1979	37
Cincinnati	Clay Carroll	1972	37
Houston	Dave Smith	1986	33
Los Angeles	Jim Brewer	1970	24
Montreal	Jeff Reardon	1985	41
New York	Jesse Orosco	1984	31
Philadelphia	Al Holland	1984	29
Philadelphia	Steve Bedrosian	1986	29
Pittsburgh	Kent Tekulve	1979	31
St. Louis	Bruce Sutter	1984	45
San Diego	Rollie Fingers	1978	37
San Francisco	Greg Minton	1982	30

Fewest Passed Balls, Season, 100 or More Games

In sandlot baseball there usually is a backstop behind home plate. In major-league baseball the only backstop is the catcher. If the ball gets past the catcher, it rolls all the way to the stands. Therefore, one important role of the man in the iron mask is to keep the ball in play.

In the history of the game only four catchers have gone through a season, playing at least 100 games, and not given up a passed ball! This incredibly difficult task was last accomplished by Johnny Bench while playing for the 1975 Cincinnati Reds. The other catchers who completed a perfect season were Al Todd, Al Lopez, and New York Yankee great Bill Dickey.

FEWEST PASSED BALLS, SEASON, 100 OR MORE GAMES
AMERICAN LEAGUE

PLAYER	TEAM	PASSED BALLS	GAMES	YEAR
Bill Dickey	New York	0	125	1931
Jim Hegan	Cleveland	4	152	1949
Carlton Fisk	Boston	4	151	1977

NATIONAL LEAGUE

PLAYER	TEAM	PASSED BALLS	GAMES	YEAR
Al Todd	Pittsburgh	0	128	1937
Al Lopez	Pittsburgh	0	114	1941
Johnny Bench	Cincinnati	0	121	1975
Gary Carter	Montreal	1	152	1978

Gary Carter

Jim Hegan

Carlton Fisk

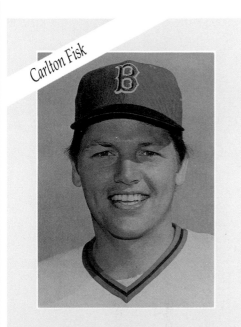

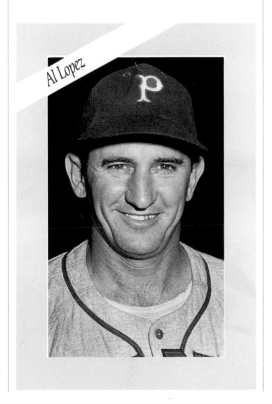

Al Lopez

RIGHT: Bill Dickey

Highest Fielding Percentage by Position, Season

A ny fan of the game knows that shortstops and first basemen field more chances than any other position. Traditionally, first basemen are also expected to provide some power in the batting line-up, whereas shortstops are known primarily for their gloves. Only recently, with players like Cal Ripken and Hubie Brooks, have shortstops begun to hit the long ball.

One shortstop, during his stint with the Texas Rangers, made baseball history by playing every inning of a double-header without making a putout or an assist. On June 26, 1976, Toby Harrah played 18 innings of baseball at shortstop and never had to field the ball. But the day was not a total loss for Harrah. During the doubleheader he smacked two homers and drove in eight runs. On the other end of the spectrum is shortstop Eddie Joost of the 1941 Cincinnati Reds, who fielded 19 balls in a game, combining for nine putouts and ten assists.

Speaking of shortstops, Larry Bowa set a major-league record by fielding at a .991 clip in 146 games during the 1979 season. This helped lead him to the all-time career mark for shortstops – .980.

Bobby Grich

Randy Jones

BELOW: Catcher Yogi Berra had a fielding percentage of 1.00 in the 1958 season.

HIGHEST FIELDING PERCENTAGE BY POSITION, SEASON

AMERICAN LEAGUE

PLAYER	TEAM	YEAR	POS.	PERCENTAGE
Stuffy McInnis	BOS	1921	1B	.999
Bobby Grich	BAL	1973	2B	.995
Don Money	MIL	1974	3B	.989
Ed Brinkman	DET	1972	SS	.990
Rocky Colavito	KC	1964	OF	1.000
Mickey Stanley	DET	1968	OF	1.000
Mickey Stanley	DET	1970	OF	1.000
Roy White	NY	1971	OF	1.000
Ken Berry	CAL	1972	OF	1.000
Carl Yastrzemski	BOS	1977	OF	1.000
Buddy Rosar	PHI	1946	C	1.000
Lou Berberet	WAS	1957	C	1.000
Pete Daley	BOS	1957	C	1.000
Yogi Berra	NY	1958	C	1.000
Walter Johnson	WAS	1913	P	1.000

NATIONAL LEAGUE

PLAYER	TEAM	YEAR	POS.	PERCENTAGE
Frank McCormick	PHI	1946	1B	.999
Red Schoendienst	STL	1956	1B	.999
Red Schoendienst	NY	1956	2B	.993
Heinie Groh	NY	1924	3B	.983
Larry Bowa	PHI	1979	SS	.991
Danny Litwhiler	PHI	1942	OF	1.000
Tony Gonzalez	PHI	1962	OF	1.000
Curt Flood	STL	1966	OF	1.000
Terry Puhl	HOU	1979	OF	1.000
Wes Westrum	NY	1950	C	.999
Randy Jones	SD	1976	P	1.000

LEFT: Terry Puhl

BELOW: Ed Brinkman hopes to put out Davey Johnson.

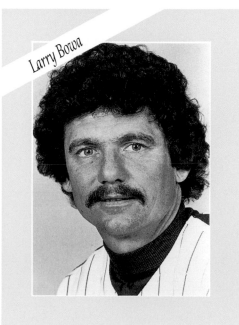

Larry Bowa

Fewest Putouts at First Base, Nine-Inning Game

In baseball lore, the ground ball has been called the pitcher's best friend. Nothing frustrates a hitter more than bouncing the ball to an eager infielder who deftly tosses it to first.

Since the ground ball is such a common event in a game, it's surprising to find that sometimes the first baseman never makes a putout. In fact, since it takes 27 outs per nine-inning game, most first basemen get many chances to touch the bag in front of the charging runner. In the history of the game, only ten first basemen have had the luxury of recording the fewest putouts in a nine-inning game. Members of this unusual group might just as well have stayed in the dugout and taken the day off.

The latest first baseman to record zero putouts in a game was Len Matuszek, playing for the Philadelphia Phillies in 1984. Others on the meager list include Frank Robinson, Gene Tenace, and Dolph Camilli.

FEWEST PUTOUTS AT FIRST BASE, NINE-INNING GAME

NATIONAL LEAGUE

PLAYER	TEAM	PUTOUTS	YEAR
Jim Collins	St. Louis	0	1935
Jim Collins	Chicago	0	1937
Dolph Camilli	Philadelphia	0	1937
Earl Torgeson	Boston	0	1947
Gary Thomasson	San Francisco	0	1977
Len Matuszek	Philadelphia	0	1984

AMERICAN LEAGUE

PLAYER	TEAM	PUTOUTS	YEAR
John Clancy	Chicago	0	1930
Rudy York	Detroit	0	1943
Frank Robinson	Baltimore	0	1971
Gene Tenace	Oakland	0	1974

Dolph Camilli

Rudy York

BELOW: *Frank Robinson (right) chats with Ed Matlock.*

ABOVE: *Earl Torgeson*

Most Years Leading League in Double Plays, Second Baseman

The old adage is that for a team to have a winning season, it must be strong up the middle. For fielders, that includes the catcher, center fielder, shortstop, and the second baseman. Second basemen are an integral part of the infield double play. Whether starting the play by fielding the ground ball or grabbing the relay, the second baseman must be blessed with agility and speed.

Bill Mazeroski of the Pittsburgh Pirates holds the record for leading the league in double plays for the most years. From 1960 through 1967, Mazeroski led the National League a remarkable eight times!

Sharing the American League's mark of five seasons are Nap Lajoie, Eddie Collins, Stan Harris, Bob Doerr, and Nellie Fox.

BELOW: Ed Collins

RIGHT: Nellie Fox

MOST YEARS LEADING LEAGUE IN DOUBLE PLAYS, SECOND BASEMAN

AMERICAN LEAGUE

PLAYER	TEAM	YEARS
Nap Lajoie	Cleveland	1903, 1906, 1907, 1908, 1909
Ed Collins	Philadelphia	1909, 1910, 1912, 1916, 1919
Stan Harris	Washington	1921, 1922, 1923, 1924, 1925
Bob Doerr	Boston	1938, 1940, 1943, 1946, 1947
Nellie Fox	Chicago	1954, 1956, 1957, 1958, 1960

NATIONAL LEAGUE

PLAYER	TEAM	YEARS
Bill Mazeroski	Pittsburgh	1960, 1961, 1962, 1963, 1964, 1965, 1966, 1967

Bobby Doerr

Most Years Leading League in Fielding, 100 or More Games, Shortstop

F or years the position of shortstop was limited to one-dimensional players – those gifted more with the glove than the bat. Although players like Cal Ripken and Alan Trammell have changed that image, it's still a thrill to watch some of the game's greatest glovemen make the plays at short.

In the American League Everett Scott, Lou Boudreau, and Luis Aparicio hold the record for most years leading the league in fielding. These players each led the rest of the pack eight times.

In the National League, Larry Bowa, playing for the Phillies and the Cubs, led the league six times.

Some of today's top-fielding shortstops include Ozzie Smith of the St. Louis Cardinals and sure-handed Tony Fernandez of the Toronto Blue Jays.

RIGHT: *Shortstop Luis Aparicio led the league in fielding for eight years.*

MOST YEARS LEADING LEAGUE IN FIELDING, 100 OR MORE GAMES, SHORTSTOP

PLAYER	TEAM	YEARS
Everett Scott	Boston AL	1916
		1917
		1918
		1919
		1920
		1921
		1922
		1923
Lou Boudreau	Cleveland AL	1940
		1941
		1942
		1943
		1944
		1946
		1947
		1948
Luis Aparicio	Chicago AL and Baltimore AL	1959
		1960
		1961
		1962
		1963
		1964
		1965
		1966
Larry Bowa	Philadelphia NL and Chicago NL	1971
		1972
		1974
		1978
		1979
		1983

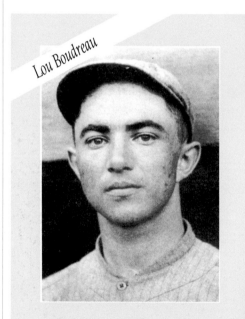

Lou Boudreau

Everett Scott

Most Assists in a Season, Third Baseman

B aseball fans refer to third base as "the hot corner." Not only do runners race around that bag toward home, but for a fielder playing that position, at times it must be like catching flying bullets! How many times has a third baseman thrilled the crowd by making a diving catch of a ball sent blistering toward the outfield grass? In fact, fielding third base is so difficult that many players get standing ovations just for knocking down the ball.

The all-time record holder for most assists in a season by a third baseman in a 162-game schedule is held by Graig Nettles. In 1971, Nettles, while a member of the Cleveland Indians, recorded an incredible 412 assists!

The National League mark by guardians of the hot corner is held by Mike Schmidt of the 1974 Philadelphia Phillies. Schmidt nailed down 404 assists during that busy season.

NATIONAL LEAGUE				
PLAYER	TEAM	ASSISTS	GAMES	YEAR
Mike Schmidt	Philadelphia	404	162	1974
Bill Shindle	Baltimore	384	134	1892
Tom Leach	Pittsburgh	371	146	1904

MOST ASSISTS IN A SEASON, THIRD BASEMAN

AMERICAN LEAGUE				
PLAYER	TEAM	ASSISTS	GAMES	YEAR
Graig Nettles	Cleveland	412	158	1971
Harlond Clift	St Louis	405	155	1937

Horlond Clift

RIGHT: *Veteran third baseman Graig Nettles holds the record for most assists in a season – an amazing 412!*

Highest Outfielder Fielding Average, Season, 100 or More Games

S ometimes when you look at an outfielder it seems as if he does little more than watch the grass grow and occasionally catch a lazy fly ball. However, when the ball is smacked to the gaps and the action heats up, the outfielders are put to the task of cutting the ball and the runner down.

Since errors can occur at any point while catching or throwing the baseball, most outfielders are content to finish the season with ten errors or less. Considering the typical grueling schedule of cross-continent travel and day games following night contests, very few outfielders play a whole season unscathed.

However, some outfielders have gone through an entire season without making an error. The last outfielder to accomplish this feat was Brian Downing with the 1984 California Angels. Some other members of the perfect fielding club include Carl Yastrzemski, Terry Puhl, Roy White, Al Kaline, and Curt Flood.

Brian Downing

Al Kaline

ABOVE: *Dan Litwhiler demonstrates the form that gave him the highest fielding average for an outfielder in 1942.*

HIGHEST OUTFIELDER FIELDING AVERAGE, SEASON, 100 OR MORE GAMES

AMERICAN LEAGUE

PLAYER	TEAM	AVE.	GAMES	YEAR
Rocco Colavito	Cleveland	1.00	162	1965
Russ Snyder	Baltimore	1.00	106	1965
Bud Harrelson	Boston	1.00	132	1968
Mitch Stanley	Detroit	1.00	130	1968
Kent Berry	Chicago	1.00	120	1969
Mitch Stanley	Detroit	1.00	132	1970
Roy White	New York	1.00	145	1971
Al Kaline	Detroit	1.00	129	1971
Kent Berry	California	1.00	116	1972
Carl Yastrzemski	Boston	1.00	140	1977
Billy Sample	Texas	1.00	103	1979
Gary Roenicke	Baltimore	1.00	113	1980
Bob Clark	California	1.00	102	1982
Brian Downing	California	1.00	158	1982
John Lowenstein	Baltimore	1.00	112	1982
Brian Downing	California	1.00	131	1984

NATIONAL LEAGUE

PLAYER	TEAM	AVE.	GAMES	YEAR
Dan Litwhiler	Philadelphia	1.00	151	1942
Will Marshall	Boston	1.00	136	1951
Tony Gonzalez	Philadelphia	1.00	114	1962
Don Demeter	Philadelphia	1.00	119	1963
Curt Flood	St. Louis	1.00	159	1966
John Callison	Philadelphia	1.00	109	1968
Terry Puhl	Houston	1.00	152	1979
Gary Woods	Chicago	1.00	103	1982

Unassisted Triple Plays

O ne of the rarest and most memorable events in baseball is the unassisted triple play. It's one of those "bang-bang" happenings that stuns both the runners and the team in the field. There have only been eight unassisted triple plays in baseball history, all made with the runners on first and second.

Obviously, the first out is a hard-hit liner to one of the infielders. The runners, thinking the ball is a base hit, break for second and third. The quick-thinking fielder races to tag the runner or step on second base before attempting the third out.

The last unassisted triple play was performed by Ron Hansen, shortstop for the Washington Senators, in 1968. In the first inning against Cleveland on July 30, Hansen thrilled the fans with his feat, while many spectators were still finding their seats.

UNASSISTED TRIPLE PLAYS

PLAYER	POSITION	TEAM	YEAR
Neal Ball	shortstop	Indians	1909
Bill Wambsganns	second base	Indians	1920
George Burns	first base	Red Sox	1923
Ernie Padgett	shortstop	Boston Braves	1923
Glenn Wright	shortstop	Pirates	1925
Jim Cooney	shortstop	Cubs	1927
John Neun	first base	Tigers	1927
Ron Hansen	shortstop	Senators	1968

Bill Wambsganss

BELOW: George Burns

Glenn Wright

The Elusive 200-20-20-20-20 Club

With all the statistics available it's not too surprising that baseball fans, through various combinations, always come up with a few more. Recently, there has been discussion of the elusive 200–20–20–20–20 club. No player in baseball history has ever had a season when he had 200 or more hits plus 20 or more doubles, triples, homers, and stolen bases.

Of all the players, only Ryne Sandberg of the Chicago Cubs has come close. During the 1984 season, Sandberg came the closest to achieving that plateau, falling short by only one triple and one home run. Looking at the list of the top six in this category, you'll see some very familiar names, like Willie Mays and George Brett, and some less-than-famous types, like Jim Bottomly. Surprisingly, Bottomly was inducted into the Hall of Fame in 1974 for his exploits during his 16-year career.

THE ELUSIVE 200–20–20–20–20

PLAYER	YEAR	TEAM	HITS	2B	3B	HR	SB
Ryne Sandberg	1984	Cubs	200	36	19	19	32
Willie Mays	1957	Giants	195	26	20	35	38
George Brett	1980	Royals	212	42	20	23	17
Jeff Heath	1941	Indians	199	32	20	24	18
Jim Bottomley	1925	Browns	227	42	20	31	10
Frank Schulte	1911	Cubs	173	30	21	21	23

BELOW: *George Brett*

Jeff Heath

BELOW: *Ryne Sandberg*

Most Games Played

E very boy dreams of someday playing in the major leagues. Some of the lucky ones grow up and get signed to a professional contract. Then, after battling the odds in the minors, they get the call and play in their first Major League game. Most of these players last a few years and then call it a career. But the very fortunate get to play "the summer game" for many years.

Like so many other records in his possession, Pete Rose holds the all-time record for having played in the most games. Pete suited up for 3,562 games during his illustrious career. With the advent of modern medicine and training practices, many of the players on the list have been active within the past 20 years. Rusty Staub, Hank Aaron, and Carl Yastrzemski all completed their career only after piling up the games played.

George Davis	2370	.297
Rod Wallace	2369	.267
Al Oliver	2368	.303
Nellie Fox	2367	.288
Willie Stargell	2360	.282
Bert Campaneris	2328	.259
Charlie Gehringer	2323	.320
Jimmy Foxx	2317	.325
Frank Frisch	2311	.316
Harry Hooper	2308	.281
Steve Garvey	2305	.295
Ted Simmons	2305	.286
Dave Concepcion	2300	.267

MOST GAMES PLAYED

PLAYER	GAMES	AVERAGE
Pete Rose	3562	.303
Carl Yastrzemski	3308	.285
Henry Aaron	3298	.305
Ty Cobb	3033	.367
Stan Musial	3026	.331
Willie Mays	2992	.302
Rusty Staub	2951	.279
Brooks Robinson	2896	.267
Al Kaline	2834	.297
Eddie Collins	2826	.333
Frank Robinson	2808	.294
Tris Speaker	2790	.345
Honus Wagner	2785	.329
Tony Perez	2777	.279
Mel Ott	2730	.304
Reggie Jackson	2705	.263
Rabbit Maranville	2670	.258
Joe Morgan	2649	.271
Lou Brock	2616	.293
Luis Aparicio	2599	.262
Willie McCovey	2588	.270
Paul Waner	2549	.333
Ernie Banks	2528	.274
Graig Nettles	2508	.249
Sam Crawford	2505	.309
Babe Ruth	2503	.342
Billy Williams	2488	.290
Nap Lajoie	2475	.339
Max Carey	2469	.285
Vada Pinson	2469	.286
Rod Carew	2469	.328
Ron Fairly	2442	.266
Harmon Killebrew	2435	.256
Roberto Clemente	2433	.317
Bill Dahlen	2431	.275
Willie Davis	2429	.279
Luke Appling	2422	.310
Jim Vernon	2409	.286
Zack Wheat	2406	.317
Ed Rice	2404	.322
Mickey Mantle	2401	.298
Eddie Mathews	2391	.271
Enos Slaughter	2380	.300
Jake Beckley	2373	.309

Carl Yastrzemski

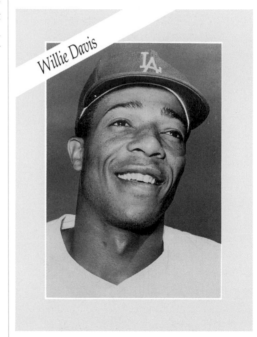

Willie Davis

Pete Rose

LEFT: A youthful Pete Rose begins his career in 1963; he retired 3,562 games later.

ABOVE: Babe Ruth retires from baseball after 2,503 games.

500 Consecutive Games Played

The iron men of the game were those who could suit up for play regardless of injuries or fatigue. The sturdiest player had to be Lou Gehrig, who played in 2,130 consecutive games, a record that many feel will never be broken. Today, with the elongated season and day games following night games, the increased wear and tear on ballplayers requires them to get some rest. Consider the fact that for a player to break Gehrig's record he would have to play in every game for over 13 consecutive seasons!

Of the players on the list, Pete Rose and Charlie Gehringer distinguished themselves by having two streaks. As for one consecutive streak, Steve Garvey, while playing for the Dodgers and the Padres, put together 1,207 games to capture third place on the list. Of today's ballplayers, Baltimore's Cal Ripken is the new Iron Man, with over 927 consecutive games under his belt.

500 Consecutive Games Played

PLAYER	GAMES
Lou Gehrig	2,130
Everett Scott	1,307
Steve Garvey	1,207
Billy Williams	1,117
Joe Sewell	1,103
Cal Ripken	927
Stan Musial	895
Ed Yost	829
Gus Suhr	822
Nellie Fox	798
Pete Rose	745
Dale Murphy	740
Richie Ashburn	730
Ernie Banks	717
Pete Rose	678
Earl Averill	673
Frank McCormick	652
Sandy Alomar	648
Ed Brown	618
Roy McMillan	585
George Pinckney	577
Walter Brodie	574
Aaron Ward	565
George LaChance	540
John Freeman	535
Fred Luderus	533
Clyde Milan	511
Charlie Gehringer	511
Vada Pinson	508
Tony Cuccinello	504
Charlie Gehringer	504
Omar Moreno	503

RIGHT: Gary Cooper played the role of Lou Gehrig in the film Pride of the Yankees. Gehrig played 2,130 games in a row before illness forced him to retire.

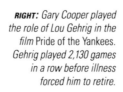

ABOVE RIGHT: Steve Garvey

Most Games in a Rookie Season

I t is the dream of every minor-league player to someday make it to the majors. Most are content to play in the tail end of lopsided games that first season in the big leagues. But a few rookies have somehow found a way to play in every game.

Thirteen rookies have played every game during their first season. While such notables as Tony Lazzeri, Harvey Kuenn, and Al Rosen accomplished the task during the 154-game schedule, a few players were also able to run the season in the 162-game format.

In the American League, Jacob Wood, Bobby Knoop, and George Scott played every game during their rookie years. Over in the National League, the job was performed by Dick Allen and Johnny Ray.

MOST GAMES IN A ROOKIE SEASON
AMERICAN LEAGUE

PLAYER	GAMES	TEAM	YEAR
Jake Wood	162	Detroit	1961
Bobby Knoop	162	Los Angeles	1964
George Scott	162	Boston	1966
Billy Rigney	155	Detroit	1922
Tony Lazzeri	155	New York	1926
Dale Alexander	155	Detroit	1929
Bill Johnson	155	New York	1943
Dick Wakefield	155	Detroit	1943
Al Rosen	155	Cleveland	1950
Harvey Kuenn	155	Detroit	1953

NATIONAL LEAGUE

PLAYER	GAMES	TEAM	YEAR
Richie Allen	162	Philadelphia	1964
Johnny Ray	162	Pittsburgh	1982
Ray Jablonski	157	St. Louis	1953

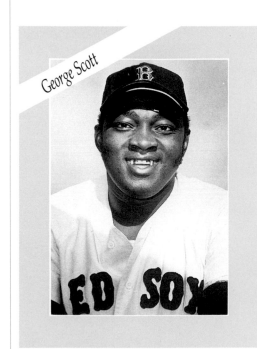

George Scott

RIGHT: *Bobby Knoop leaps to make the catch and put the tag on. Knoop played 162 games in his rookie season.*

Directly to the Majors

Since the start of the amateur free-agent draft in 1965, only 14 players have made their professional debut in the major leagues. These players were able to crack the major-league lineup without the benefit of any minor league experience. It is a ballplayer's dream to skip the long bus rides and tedious routine of the minor leagues. To start on the major-league level takes skill and a lot of lucky timing. For example, Pete Incaviglia of the Texas Rangers was lucky enough to be blessed with long-ball talent and to be drafted by a team willing to take a chance. Nobody expected the Texas Rangers to launch a challenge during the 1985 campaign, so Manager Bobby Valentine was willing to take a chance with "the kid". Incaviglia responded by belting 30 home runs and driving in 88 men. His power is so awesome that on October 1, 1985 he hit a sacrifice fly so far that it drove in two runs!

Bringing a player along too quickly can have dire consequences. Some players, like pitcher David Clyde, never get the chance to develop and have short careers. Others, like Dave Winfield, flourish in the big time and continue to wallop the ball for years.

Rookie superstar Pete Incaviglia went directly to the majors in 1985.

DIRECTLY TO THE MAJORS

PLAYER	POSITION	YEAR	TEAM
Mike Adamson	P	1967	Baltimore
Steve Dunning	P	1969	Cleveland
Pete Broberg	P	1971	Washington
Burt Hooton	P	1971	Chicago NL
Dave Roberts	3B	1972	San Diego
Dick Ruthven	P	1973	Philadelphia
David Clyde	P	1973	Texas
Dave Winfield	OF	1973	San Diego
Eddie Bane	P	1973	Minnesota
Bob Horner	3B	1978	Atlanta
Brian Milner	C	1978	Toronto
Mike Morgan	P	1978	Oakland
Tim Conroy	P	1978	Oakland
Pete Incaviglia	OF	1985	Texas

RIGHT: Mike Morgan

Burt Hooton

Most Days in First Place, Season

At the beginning of the season, a team leaves spring training hoping to get off on the right foot with some wins. A few teams get that first win and never stumble.

In 1984, the Detroit Tigers had the ultimate dream season. From the first pitch of opening day to the final out of the season, the Tigers were never out of first place. Sparky Anderson's team set a major-league record by being in or tied for first place for 181 days. During that span, they held sole position on top of the American League East for 176 days.

Some other pennant winners didn't have that luxury. In 1967, the Boston Red Sox spent only 20 days in first and only six of those days in sole possession!

MOST DAYS IN FIRST PLACE, SEASON

TEAM	DAYS	YEAR	COMMENT
Detroit AL	181	1984	5 days tied, 176 days alone; 162-game season
Cincinnati NL	178	1970	all season except 11 April; 162-game season
New York NL	174	1923	all season except 17 April, tied; 154-game season
New York AL	174	1927	8 days tied, 166 days alone; 154-game season

RIGHT: *John McGraw managed the Giants to 174 days in first place in 1923.*

Longest Game in Innings

There's nothing like a day at the ballpark. But sometimes that day turns into night, putting a strain on players and fans alike. The fans really feel they're getting their money's worth during an extra-inning ballgame. However, when that scoreboard starts to expand, and the game enters the 13th or 14th inning, you wish somebody would break the deadlock so everyone can go home. Exasperated managers, running short on players, begin shuffling their line-ups, using any available body. Relief pitchers are forced to throw the equivalent of a regulation game.

The longest game in history took place in Boston on May 1, 1920. In a game lasting 26 innings, Brooklyn and Boston played to a 1–1 tie.

In the American League, the Chicago White Sox and the Milwaukee Brewers battled for 25 innings in a game played on consecutive days. They began the game on May 8, 1984, played 17 innings, and then finished on May 9. Chicago survived with a 7–6 win.

LONGEST GAME IN INNINGS
AMERICAN LEAGUE

25 INNINGS
Chicago 7, Milwaukee 6, 8 May, 1984 (17 innings), finished 9 May, 1984 (8 innings), at Chicago

24 INNINGS
Philadelphia 4, Boston 1, 1 September, 1906 at Boston
Detroit 1, Philadelphia 1 (tie), 21 July, 1945 at Philadelphia

22 INNINGS
New York 9, Detroit 7, 24 June, 1962 at Detroit
Washington 6, Chicago 5, 12 June, 1967 at Washington
Milwaukee 4, Minnesota 3, 12 May, 1972 (21 innings), finished 13 May, 1972 (1 inning) at Minnesota

21 INNINGS
Detroit 6, Chicago 5, 24 May, 1929 at Chicago
Oakland 5, Washington 3, 4 June, 1971 at Washington
Chicago 6, Cleveland 3, 26 May, 1973, finished 28 May, 1973 at Chicago

20 INNINGS
Philadelphia 4, Boston 2, 4 July, 1905 at Boston
Washington 9, Minnesota 7, 9 August, 1967 at Minnesota
New York 4, Boston 3, 29 August, 1967, second game, at New York
Boston 5, Seattle 3, 27 July, 1969 at Seattle
Oakland 1, California 0, 9 July, 1971 at Oakland
Washington 8, Cleveland 6, 14 Sept, 1971, second game (16 innings), finished 20 Sept, 1971 (4 innings), started at Cleveland, finished at Washington
Seattle 8, Boston 7, 3 Sept, 1981 (19 innings), finished 4 Sept, 1981 (1 inning) at Boston
California 4, Seattle 3, 13 April, 1982 (17 innings), finished 14 April, 1982 (3 innings), at California

19 INNINGS
Washington 5, Philadelphia 4, 27 Sept, 1912 at Philadelphia
Chicago 5, Cleveland 4, 24 June, 1915 at Cleveland
Cleveland 3, New York 2, 24 May, 1918 at New York
St Louis 8, Washington 6, 9 August, 1921 at Washington
Chicago 5, Boston 4, 13 July, 1951 at Chicago
Cleveland 4, St. Louis 3, 1 July, 1952 at Cleveland
Cleveland 3, Washington 2, 14 June, 1963, second game at Cleveland

Baltimore 7, Washington 5, 4 June, 1967 at Baltimore
Kansas City 6, Detroit 5, 17 June, 1967, second game, at Detroit
Detroit 3, New York 3 (tie), 23 August, 1968, second game, at New York
Oakland 5, Chicago 3, 10 August, 1972 (17 innings), finished 11 August, 1972 (2 innings), at Oakland
New York 5, Minnesota 4, 25 August, 1976, at New York
Cleveland 8, Detroit 4, 27 April, 1984, at Detroit

18 INNINGS
Chicago 6, New York 6 (tie), 25 June, 1903 at Chicago
Washington 0, Detroit 0 (tie), 16 July, 1909 at Detroit
Washington 1, Chicago 0, 15 May, 1918 at Washington
Detroit 7, Washington 6, 4 August, 1918 at Detroit
Boston 12, New York 11, 5 September, 1927, first game, at Boston
Philadelphia 18, Cleveland 17, 10 July, 1932 at Cleveland
New York 3, Chicago 3 (tie), 21 August, 1933 at Chicago
Washington 1, Chicago 0, 8 June, 1947, first game, at Chicago
Washington 5, St Louis 5 (tie), 20 June 1952 at St Louis
Chicago 1, Baltimore 1 (tie), 6 August, 1959 at Baltimore
New York 7, Boston 6, 16 April, 1967 at New York
Minnesota 3, New York 2, 26 July, 1967, second game, at New York
Baltimore 3, Boston 2, 25 August, 1968 at Baltimore
Minnesota 11, Seattle 7, 19 July, 1969 (16 innings), finished 20 July, 1969 (2 innings), at Seattle
Oakland 9, Baltimore 8, 24 August, 1969, second game, at Oakland
Minnesota 8, Oakland 6, 6 Sept, 1969 at Oakland
Washington 2, New York 1, 22 April, 1970 at Washington
Texas 4, Kansas City 3, 17 May, 1972 at Kansas City
Detroit 4, Cleveland 3, 9 June, 1982 (14 innings), finished 24 Sept, 1982 (4 innings), at Detroit

NATIONAL LEAGUE

26 INNINGS
Brooklyn 1, Boston 1 (tie), 1 May, 1920 at Boston

25 INNINGS
St. Louis 4, New York 3, 11 Sept, 1974 at New York

24 INNINGS
Houston 1, New York 0, 15 April, 1968 at Houston

23 INNINGS
Brooklyn 2, Boston 2 (tie), 27 June, 1939 at Boston
San Francisco 8, New York 6, 31 May, 1964, second game at New York

22 INNINGS
Brooklyn 6, Pittsburgh 5, 22 August, 1917 at Brooklyn
Chicago 4, Boston 3, 17 May, 1927 at Boston

21 INNINGS
New York 3, Pittsburgh 1, 17 July, 1914 at Pittsburgh
Chicago 2, Philadelphia 1, 17 July, 1918 at Chicago
Pittsburgh 2, Boston 0, 1 August, 1918 at Boston
San Francisco 1, Cincinnati 0, 1 Sept, 1967 at Cincinnati
Houston 2, San Diego 1, 24 Sept, 1971, first game, at San Diego
San Diego 11, Montreal 8, 21 May, 1977 at Montreal
Los Angeles 2, Chicago 1, 17 Aug, 1982 (17 innings), finished 18 Aug, 1982 (4 innings), at Chicago

20 INNINGS
Chicago 7, Cincinnati 7 (tie), 30 June, 1892 at Cincinnati
Chicago 2, Philadelphia 1, 24 August, 1905 at Philadelphia
Brooklyn 9, Philadelphia 9 (tie), 30 April, 1919 at Philadelphia
St. Louis 8, Chicago 7, 28 August, 1930 at Chicago
Brooklyn 6, Boston 2, 5 July, 1940 at Boston
Philadelphia 5, Atlanta 4, 4 May, 1973 at Philadelphia
Pittsburgh 5, Chicago 4, 6 July, 1980 at Pittsburgh
Houston 3, San Diego 1, 15 August, 1980 at San Diego

19 INNINGS
Chicago 3, Pittsburgh 2, 22 June, 1902 at Chicago
Pittsburgh 7, Boston 6, 31 July, 1912 at Boston
Chicago 4, Brooklyn 3, 17 June, 1915 at Chicago
St. Louis 8, Philadelphia 8 (tie), 13 June, 1918 at Philadelphia
Boston 2, Brooklyn 1, 3 May, 1920 at Boston

Chicago 3, Boston 2, 17 August, 1932 at Chicago
Brooklyn 9, Chicago 9 (tie), 17 May, 1939 at Chicago
Cincinnati 0, Brooklyn 0 (tie), 11 Sept, 1946 at Brooklyn
Philadelphia 8, Cincinnati 7, 15 Sept, 1950, second game, at Philadelphia
Pittsburgh 4, Milwaukee 3, 19 July, 1955 at Pittsburgh
Cincinnati 2, Los Angeles 1, 8 August, 1972 at Cincinnati
New York 7, Los Angeles 3, 24 May, 1973 at Los Angeles
Pittsburgh 4, San Diego 3, 25 August, 1979 at San Diego
New York 16, Atlanta 13, 4 July, 1985 at Atlanta
Montreal 6, Houston 3, 7 July, 1985 at Houston

18 INNINGS
Providence 1, Detroit 0, 17 August, 1882 at Providence
Brooklyn 7, St Louis 7 (tie), 17 August, 1902 at St Louis
Chicago 2, St Louis 1, 24 June, 1905 at St Louis
Pittsburgh 3, Chicago 2, 28 June, 1916, second game, at Chicago
Philadelphia 10, Brooklyn 9, 1 June, 1919 at Brooklyn
New York 9, Pittsburgh 8, 7 July, 1922 at Pittsburgh
Chicago 7, Boston 2, 14 May, 1927 at Boston
New York 1, St Louis 0, 2 July, 1933, first game, at New York
St. Louis 8, Cincinnati 6, 1 July, 1934, first game, at Cincinnati
Chicago 10, Cincinnati 8, 9 August, 1942, first game, at Cincinnati
Philadelphia 4, Pittsburgh 3, 9 June, 1949 at Philadelphia
Cincinnati 7, Chicago 6, 7 Sept, 1951 at Cincinnati
Philadelphia 0, New York 0 (tie), 2 Oct, 1965, second game, at New York
Cincinnati 3, Chicago 2, 19 July, 1966 at Chicago
Philadelphia 2, Cincinnati 1, 21 May, 1967 at Philadelphia
Pittsburgh 1, San Diego 0, 7 June, 1972, second game, at San Diego
New York 3, Philadelphia 2, 1 August, 1972, first game, at New York
Montreal 5, Chicago 4, 27 June, 1973, finished 28 June, 1973 at Chicago
Chicago 8, Montreal 7, 28 June, 1974, first game, at Montreal
New York 4, Montreal 3, 16 Sept, 1975 at New York
Pittsburgh 2, Chicago 1, 10 August, 1977 at Pittsburgh
Chicago 9, Cincinnati 8, 10 May, 1979, finished 23 July at Chicago
Houston 3, New York 2, 18 June, 1979 at Houston
San Diego 8, New York 6, 26 August, 1980 at New York
St Louis 3, Houston 1, 27 May, 1983 at Houston
Pittsburgh 4, San Francisco 3, 13 July, 1984, second game, at Pittsburgh
Atlanta 3, Los Angeles 2, 6 Sept, 1984 at Los Angeles
New York 5, Pittsburgh 4, 28 April, 1985 at New York
San Francisco 5, Atlanta 4, 11 June, 1985 at Atlanta
Houston 8, Chicago 7, 2 Sept, 1986 (14 innings), finished 3 Sept, 1986 (4 innings) at Chicago

Most Years with One Team

In today's modern baseball world of trades and free agency, rarely does a player spend most, if not all, of his career with the same team. But some players were either too good or too popular to be traded. Think of today's game and try to imagine the outcry if the Yankees traded Don Mattingly or the New York Mets gave up on Dwight Gooden!

The all-time record-holders for having played the most years with one team are Brooks Robinson and Carl Yastrzemski. For 23 years, from 1955 through 1977, Brooks Robinson thrilled Baltimore Oriole fans with his bat and amazing skill at third base. And in Beantown, Carl Yastrzemski led the Boston Red Sox from 1961 through 1983.

Over in the National League in the post-1900 era, Mel Ott of the New York Giants and the St. Louis Cardinals' Stan Musial plied their trade for a remarkable 22 years with the same team.

MOST YEARS WITH ONE TEAM				
YEARS	PLAYER	TEAM	GAMES	DATES
23	Brooks Robinson	Baltimore AL	2896	1955 – 1977
23	Carl Yastrzemski	Boston AL	3308	1961 – 1983
22	Cap Anson	Chicago NL	2253	1876 – 1897
22	Mel Ott	New York NL	2730	1926 – 1947
22	Stan Musial	St. Louis NL	3026	1941 – 1963

BELOW: *Carl Yastrzemski (far left) played for the Boston Red Sox from 1961 to 1983. Carlton Fisk is at far right in this picture.*

ABOVE: *Mel Ott spent 22 years with the New York Giants.*

The Top Brothers Act: Career Hits

S ome families have all the luck and much of the talent. In the history of the game, many brothers have suited up to play ball. But how did they stack up as hitters?

As far as career hits, the Mr. and Mrs. Waner boys, Paul and Lloyd, combined for 5,611. Little wonder they were known as Big Poison and Little Poison. Next on the list come a few multiple entries. Felipe, Matty, and Jesus Alou belted out 5,094 hits. In fact, they made history by once comprising the entire outfield for the San Francisco Giants.

The DiMaggio boys, Joe, Dom and Vince, pounded 4,853 hits from their collective bats. The most numerous brothers act, though, was the Delahanty family. Ed, Jim, Frank, Joe, and Tom Delahanty ganged up for 4,211 hits.

THE TOP BROTHERS ACT: CAREER HITS

BROTHERS	HITS
Paul and Lloyd Waner	5611
Felipe, Matty and Jesus Alou	5094
Joe, Dom and Vince DiMaggio	4853
Ed, Jim, Frank, Joe and Tom Delahanty	4211
Hank and Tommy Aaron	3987
Joe and Luke Sewell	3619
Ken, Clete and Cloyd Boyer	3559
Honus and Butts Wagner	3489
Bob and Roy Johnson	3343
Emil and Bob Meusel	3214

Luke Sewell

Joe Sewell

LEFT: *Dom DiMaggio*

Emil Meusel

BELOW: Ed Delahanty

BELOW: Matty Alou

Lloyd Waner

Paul Waner

Most Clubs Played for in One Day

I t probably feels like you're the star of a bizarre science-fiction movie. You play a game for one team and some time the next day, you're playing for another! As illogical as it sounds, three players in the history of the game suited up for two teams on the same day.

Max Flack, on May 30, 1922, played for the Chicago Cubs in the morning, was traded, and played for the St. Louis Cardinals later in the day. On the flip side of that trade was Cliff Heathcote, who began the day as a Cardinal and wound up as a Cub!

The latest player to wear two hats was Joel Youngblood. Youngblood played for the Mets on August 4, 1982. After getting a hit against the Cubs, he was traded to Montreal. That afternoon he flew to Philadelphia, put on an Expo uniform and smacked a hit against the Phillies!

MOST CLUBS PLAYED FOR IN ONE DAY

PLAYER	DATE	CLUBS
Max Flack	30 May 1922	Chicago NL A.M., St Louis NL P.M.
Cliff Heathcote	30 May 1922	St. Louis NL A.M., Chicago NL P.M.
Joel Youngblood	4 August 1982	New York NL A.M., Montreal NL P.M.

LEFT: Joel Youngblood got a hit as a Met . . .

Joel Youngblood

. . . and as an Expo on the same day!

Oldest Players

T here are a few players today, such as Tommy John and Phil Niekro, who bring cheers from the crowd every time they play. Not only are they quality ballplayers, but these two represent the "old-timers" of team rosters. Still viable players in their 40s, John and Niekro make some of us believe that the fountain of youth springs eternal in baseball's locker rooms.

If playing in their 40s is an accomplishment, how about pushing it until nearly 60! Four players kept at the game well into their 50s. Leroy "Satchel" Paige pitched three innings for the Kansas City Royals at the age of 59 years, two months. Minnie Minoso belted out a pinch-hit while pushing 58. Nicholas Altrock thrilled Washington Senators fans at the age of 57. Joe Niekro finally made it into a World Series in 1987. Pitching a few innings or pinch-hitting is one thing, but imagine Jim O'Rourke, who at the age of 52, caught a complete game for the New York Giants!

OLDEST PLAYERS

PLAYER	AGE	TEAM	YEAR	POSITION
Satchel Paige	59	Kansas City AL	1965	pitcher
Minnie Minoso	57	Kansas City AL	1980	pinch hitter
Nick Altrock	57	Washington AL	1933	pinch hitter
Jim O'Rourke	52	New York AL	1904	catcher

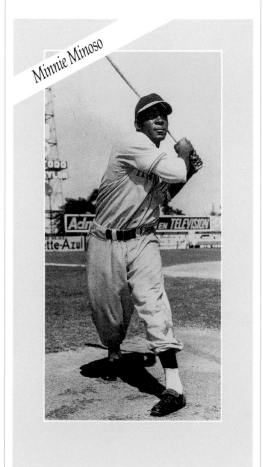

Minnie Minoso

Jim O'Rourke

RIGHT: The great Satchel Paige, one of the finest pitchers ever to play the game.

Youngest Players

There are plenty of ballplayers who keep playing the game well into their forties. Tommy John, Phil Niekro, and Pete Rose are some of the superstars who still thrill the crowds even as their hair turns gray. But the youngest player ever in the major leagues was Joe Nuxhall of the Cincinnati Reds. On June 10, 1944 Nuxhall pitched two-thirds of an inning at the tender age of 15!

Nuxhall was hammered by the St. Louis Cardinals, who roughed up the teenager for five runs. Nuxhall gave up two singles, five walks, hit one batter and left the game with an earned run average of 67.5. Although he started his career with a staggering outing, Nuxhall returned to the big leagues eight years later and wound up pitching for 16 years, compiling a won–loss record of 135–117.

Among hitters, Boston's Tony Conigliaro was the youngest teenager ever to lead a league with home runs when he pounded 32 round-trippers in 1965 at the age of 19.

Since current major league rules no longer allow the signing of ballplayers until they have graduated from high school, certain records, such as Nuxhall's achievement, will stand forever.

BELOW: Bob Feller, who began his big-league career at the tender age of 17, pitches against Joe DiMaggio.

YOUNGEST PLAYERS
AMERICAN LEAGUE

PLAYER	TEAM	FIRST YEAR	AGE
Carl Scheib	PHI	1943	16
Alex George	KC	1955	16
Jim Derrington	CHI	1956	16
Owen Shannon	STL	1903	17
Dave Skeels	DET	1910	17
Bob Williams	NY	1911	17
Merito Acosta	WAS	1913	17
Charlie Grimm	PHI	1916	17
Jimmy Foxx	PHI	1925	17
Bob Feller	CLE	1936	17
Vern Frieberger	CLE	1941	17
Bob Miller	DET	1953	17
Harmon Killebrew	WAS	1954	17

NATIONAL LEAGUE

PLAYER	TEAM	FIRST YEAR	AGE
Joe Nuxhall	CIN	1944	15
Tommy Brown	BKN	1944	16
Mike Loan	PHI	1912	17
Mel Ott	NY	1926	17
Putsy Caballero	PHI	1944	17
Granny Hamner	PHI	1944	17
Erv Palica	BKN	1945	17
Harry Chiti	CHI	1950	17
Rod Miller	BKN	1957	17
Tim McCarver	STL	1959	17
Danny Murphy	CHI	1960	17
Ed Kranepool	NY	1962	17
Jay Dahl	HOU	1963	17

Tim McCarver

BELOW: The youngest player in baseball was Joe Nuxhall, who pitched in a game in 1944 at the age of 15.

Joe Nuxhall

Most Clubs Played for, Career

No ballplayer enjoys playing on the road. Bags are packed for the three or four days in each city. Adjustments to time and climate must always be made. So pity those major leaguers who had the misfortune of being continually traded from one team to another. For these well-traveled souls, almost every ballpark felt like a second home.

Three players since 1900 have distinguished themselves by playing for ten teams during their career. For Bob Miller, the road started in St. Louis and ended 17 years later in Detroit. Tommy Davis, most noted as a Dodger, was bounced around for 18 years before retiring after 1,999 games.

George Brett's older brother Kent began his career with the Boston Red Sox in 1967 and finished 14 years later with the Kansas City Royals, his tenth team.

MOST CLUBS PLAYED FOR, CAREER

PLAYER	CLUBS	TOTAL GAMES	YEARS
Bob Miller	St. Louis New York NL Los Angeles NL Minnesota AL Cleveland AL Chicago AL Chicago NL San Diego NL Pittsburgh NL Detroit AL	807	1957 1959–1974
Tommy Davis	Los Angeles NL New York NL Chicago AL Seattle AL Houston NL Chicago NL Oakland AL Baltimore AL California AL Kansas City AL	1999	1959–1976
Ken Brett	Boston AL Milwaukee AL Philadelphia NL Pittsburgh NL New York AL Chicago AL California AL Minnesota AL Los Angeles NL Kansas City AL	349	1967 1969–1981

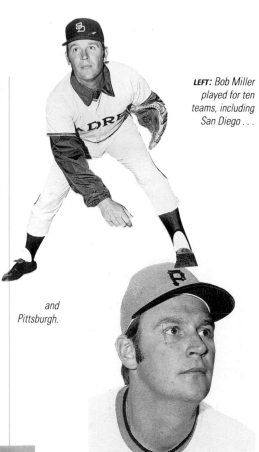

LEFT: Bob Miller played for ten teams, including San Diego . . .

and Pittsburgh.

RIGHT: Tommy Davis also played for ten teams, starting with Los Angeles and moving on to . . .

Houston . . .

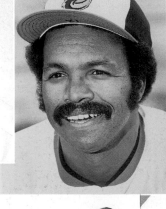

Baltimore . . .

and Kansas City.

Ken Brett played for Boston . . .

Pittsburgh . . .

Los Angeles . . .

and Kansas City.

Most Clubs as Manager, League

L ike some transient ballplayers, a few managers have made the circuit around the big leagues. It might have been a dispute with management, or poor performance by the teams, but some managers always knew to keep a travel bag packed.

Since 1900, three managers have had the distinction of being at the helm for four different National League clubs. Bill McKechnie, Rogers Hornsby, and Leo "The Lip" Durocher plied their trade in a variety of ballparks.

In the American League, James Dykes and Billy Martin each managed for five different teams. Martin also has the distinction of holding the American League record for leading one club five different times. During the 1975, 1979, 1983, 1985 and 1988 seasons, Martin put on the pinstripes to lead the New York Yankees.

MOST CLUBS AS MANAGER, LEAGUE

PLAYER	CLUBS	CLUB NAMES
Jimmy Dykes	5	Chicago AL Philadelphia AL Baltimore AL Detroit AL Cleveland AL
Billy Martin	5	Minnesota AL Detroit AL Texas AL New York AL Oakland AL
Bill McKechnie	4	Pittsburgh NL St. Louis NL Boston NL Cincinnati NL
Rogers Hornsby	4	St. Louis NL Chicago NL Boston NL Cincinnati NL
Leo Durocher	4	Brooklyn NL New York NL Chicago NL Houston NL

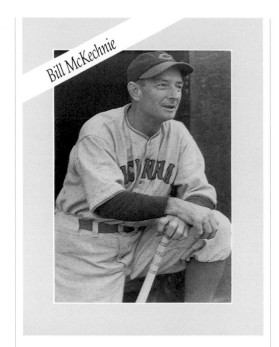

Bill McKechnie

Leo Durocher

LEFT: Jimmy Dykes

Highest World Series Batting Average

A player on a hot hitting streak can really make a difference in a limited number of games. During the regular season, a batter with a hot stick can carry his team for weeks on end. But in the World Series, when the whole baseball public watches every pitch, it's rare for one player to really shine.

However, a number of hitters have been able to put together a truly remarkable Series. For example, in a four-game Series, Babe Ruth has the highest batting average – he hit at a .625 clip during the 1928 Series. Other players, not best known for their hitting, were able to rise to the occasion to grab a piece of World Series history. Bill Martin, of the 1953 New York Yankees, batted .500.

One of the more modern players, Phil Garner of the 1979 Pittsburgh Pirates hit .500 in that seven-game Series.

HIGHEST WORLD SERIES BATTING AVERAGE

PLAYER	TEAM	GAMES	AVE	YEAR
Babe Ruth	New York AL	4	.625	1928
Larry McLean	New York NL	5	.500	1913
Joe Gordon	New York AL	5	.500	1941
Dave Robertson	New York NL	6	.500	1917
Billy Martin	New York AL	6	.500	1953
Pepper Martin	St. Louis NL	7	.500	1931
Johnny Lindell	New York AL	7	.500	1947
Phil Garner	Pittsburgh NL	7	.500	1979

Billy Martin

LEFT: Babe Ruth, holder of many batting records, also holds the record for highest batting average in a World Series.

Pepper Martin

Most Runs in a World Series

Since a team must win four games to capture the World Series, the statistics must be divided up into the actual number of games played to make any sense. But by close examination of this category, you'll see that one player, none other than Reggie Jackson, scored more runs in six games than the other leaders in the seven-game slot!

Reggie Jackson, during his memorable 1977 Series as a member of the New York Yankees, crossed home plate ten times during that six-game affair.

In seven-game series, Mickey Mantle was able to make the list twice in 1960 and 1964 by racing home eight times. At first reading, you might think that only Yankees make World Series lists. However, players such as Lou Whitaker, Lee May, and Boog Powell also used their Series adventures to distinguish themselves!

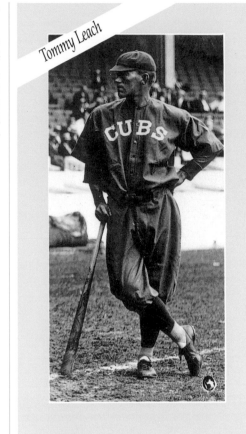
Tommy Leach

MOST RUNS IN A WORLD SERIES

PLAYER	TEAM	GAMES	RUNS	YEAR
Babe Ruth	New York AL	4	9	1928
Lou Gehrig	New York AL	4	9	1932
Frank Baker	Philadelphia AL	5	6	1910
Danny Murphy	Philadelphia AL	5	6	1910
Harry Hooper	Boston AL	5	6	1916
Al Simmons	Philadelphia AL	5	6	1929
Lee May	Cincinnati NL	5	6	1970
Boog Powell	Baltimore AL	5	6	1970
Lou Whitaker	Detroit AL	5	6	1984
Reggie Jackson	New York AL	6	10	1977
Tommy Leach	Pittsburgh NL	7	8	1909
Pepper Martin	St. Louis NL	7	8	1934
Billy Johnson	New York AL	7	8	1947
Mickey Mantle	New York AL	7	8	1960
Bobby Richardson	New York AL	7	8	1960
Mickey Mantle	New York AL	7	8	1964
Lou Brock	St. Louis NL	7	8	1967

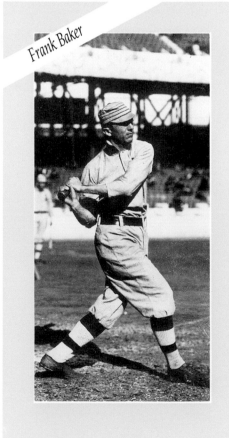
Frank Baker

ABOVE: *Boog Powell crosses the plate. Powell scored six runs in five games in the 1970 World Series.*

Most Hits in a World Series

A ballplayer's dream is to play in the October Classic. For some of the lucky ones, the hits start falling into place. The record-holders for most hits in a World Series include some Hall of Famers and a few others who made their mark for this one time only.

While sluggers like Babe Ruth, who holds the record for most hits in a four-game Series with ten, and Brooks Robinson, with nine hits in a five-game Series, made the list, others, like Paul Blair and Billy Martin, singled their way into the record books.

Fans have come to realize that sometimes the World Series is won not by the big-name players, but by the "little guy." In the most-hits category such players as Bobby Richardson, Lou Brock and Eddie Collins made their claim to fame.

BELOW: *Heinie Groh*

MOST HITS IN A WORLD SERIES

PLAYER	TEAM	GAMES	HITS	YEAR
Babe Ruth	New York AL	4	10	1928
Frank Baker	Philadelphia AL	5	9	1910
Ed Collins	Philadelphia AL	5	9	1910
Frank Baker	Philadelphia AL	5	9	1913
Heinie Groh	New York NL	5	9	1922
Joe Moore	New York NL	5	9	1937
Bobby Richardson	New York AL	5	9	1961
Paul Blair	Baltimore AL	5	9	1970
Brooks Robinson	Baltimore AL	5	9	1970
Alan Trammell	Detroit AL	5	9	1984
Billy Martin	New York AL	6	12	1953
Bobby Richardson	New York AL	7	13	1964
Lou Brock	St. Louis NL	7	13	1968

BELOW: *Frank Baker trails Babe Ruth for most hits in a World Series; he socked nine hits in five games in the 1910 Series.*

Alan Trammell

Most Home Runs in a World Series

T he ultimate feat for a batter is to smash a home run. Put that blast in a World Series game and the shot's value is magnified. For the members of this elite list, World Series homers made them an integral part of baseball history.

For a four-game Series the record-holder is Lou Gehrig, who belted his homers during the 1928 Series. Donn Clendenon smacked three homers for the New York Mets in their five-game Series in 1969.

In a six-game Series, Reggie Jackson electrified the world by pummeling the Los Angeles Dodgers in 1977.

Four players share the record for a seven-game Series. Joining Babe Ruth with four homers are Duke Snider, Hank Bauer, and Gene Tenace.

MOST HOME RUNS IN A WORLD SERIES				
PLAYER	TEAM	GAMES	HOMERS	YEAR
Lou Gehrig	New York AL	4	4	1928
Donn Clendenon	New York NL	5	3	1969
Reggie Jackson	New York AL	6	5	1977
Babe Ruth	New York AL	7	4	1926
Duke Snider	Brooklyn NL	7	4	1952
Duke Snider	Brooklyn NL	7	4	1955
Hank Bauer	New York AL	7	4	1958
Gene Tenace	Oakland AL	7	4	1972

RIGHT: Donn Clendenon

LEFT: Duke Snider twice hit four home runs in a seven-game World Series.

Players with Four or More World Series Home Runs

F or the record, certain teams really have the knack for getting into the World Series. For a long time, fans would spend the summer trying to figure out which National League team would have the dubious honor of facing the Yankees. So a quick glance of the all-time leader list in total World Series homers includes many ballplayers who donned the pin-striped uniform of the New York Yankees.

The leader of the pack is Mickey Mantle. Mantle, playing in 12 Series, belted out a total of 18 home runs. Next on the hit parade is the Sultan of Swat, Babe Ruth, who clubbed 15 homers.

Sneaking in among all those Yankee greats are superstars such as Frank Robinson, Duke Snider, Ted Simmons, and Reggie Smith.

LEFT: Bill Skowron

PLAYERS WITH FOUR OR MORE WORLD SERIES HOME RUNS

PLAYER	SERIES	HOMERS
Mickey Mantle	12	18
Babe Ruth	10	15
Yogi Berra	14	12
Duke Snider	6	11
Lou Gehrig	7	10
Reggie Jackson	5	10
Frank Robinson	5	8
Joe DiMaggio	10	8
Bill Skowron	8	8
Goose Goslin	5	7
Gil McDougald	8	7
Hank Bauer	9	7
Roger Maris	7	6
Al Simmons	4	6
Reggie Smith	4	6
Charlie Keller	4	5
Hank Greenberg	4	5
Johnny Bench	4	5
Billy Martin	5	5
Gil Hodges	7	5
Bill Dickey	8	5
Elston Howard	9	5
Tony Lazzeri	7	4
Jimmy Foxx	3	4
Mel Ott	3	4
Tommy Henrich	4	4
Joe Gordon	6	4
Roy Campanella	5	4
Joe Collins	7	4
Tom Tresh	3	4
Don Buford	3	4
Lou Brock	3	4
Gene Tenace	3	4
Davey Lopes	4	4
Willie Aikens	1	4
Steve Yeager	4	4

Most Bases on Balls in a World Series Game

T o work the count to four balls requires a keen batting eye. Perhaps some players see better in the autumn light, because they were able to set World Series records for most bases on balls in a game.

The three players who walked four times in regulation nine-inning game were Fred Clarke, Babe Ruth, and the latest – Doug DeCinces, while playing for the 1979 Baltimore Orioles.

Among the three players who set their marks in extra-inning games is Jackie Robinson, who set the world on fire while a member of the Brooklyn Dodgers.

RIGHT: *Ross Youngs*

MOST BASES ON BALLS IN A WORLD SERIES GAME				
PLAYER	TEAM	WALKS	INNINGS	YEAR
Fred Clarke	Pittsburgh NL	4	9	1909
Dick Hoblitzell	Boston AL	4	14	1916
Ross Youngs	New York NL	4	12	1924
Babe Ruth	New York NL	4	9	1926
Jackie Robinson	Brooklyn NL	4	11	1952
Doug DeCinces	Baltimore AL	4	9	1979

Fred Clarke

Most Home Runs in a World Series Game

While only Babe Ruth and Reggie Jackson have hit three home runs in a single World Series game, many players have managed to smack two over the fence. Surprisingly, more than twice as many of these players were American Leaguers!

The latest player to nail two home runs in a single World Series game was Gary Carter of the 1986 New York Mets. In 1984 two members of the Detroit Tigers, Alan Trammell and Kirk Gibson, hit two round-trippers. Some of the other players to make the list include Dave Lopes, Carl Yastrzemski, Mickey Mantle, Tony Perez, Willie McGee, and Eddie Murray.

Willie Aikens of the Kansas City Royals distinguished himself by hitting two homers in a game *twice* during the 1980 Series.

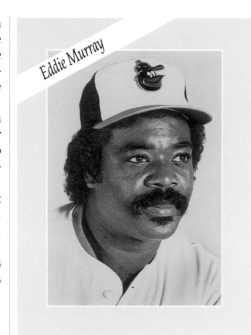

Eddie Murray

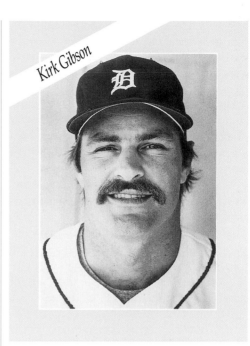

Kirk Gibson

MOST HOME RUNS IN A WORLD SERIES GAME

PLAYER	TEAM	HOMERS	YEAR
Babe Ruth	New York AL	3	1926
Babe Ruth	New York AL	3	1928
Reggie Jackson	New York AL	3*	1977
Patsy Dougherty	Boston AL	2	1903
Harry Hooper	Boston AL	2	1915
Benny Kauff	New York NL	2	1917
Babe Ruth	New York AL	2*	1923
Lou Gehrig	New York AL	2*	1928
Lou Gehrig	New York AL	2*	1932
Babe Ruth	New York AL	2	1932
Tony Lazzeri	New York AL	2	1932
Charlie Keller	New York AL	2	1939
Bob Elliott	Boston NL	2*	1948
Duke Snider	Brooklyn NL	2*	1952
Joe Collins	New York AL	2*	1955
Duke Snider	Brooklyn NL	2*	1955
Yogi Berra	New York AL	2*	1956
Tony Kubek	New York AL	2	1957
Mickey Mantle	New York AL	2	1958
Ted Kluszewski	Chicago AL	2*	1959
Charlie Neal	Los Angeles NL	2*	1959
Mickey Mantle	New York AL	2	1960
Carl Yastrzemski	Boston AL	2	1967
Rico Petrocelli	Boston AL	2*	1967
Gene Tenace	Oakland AL	2*	1972
Tony Perez	Cincinnati NL	2*	1975
Johnny Bench	Cincinnati NL	2	1976
Davy Lopes	Los Angeles NL	2*	1978
Willie Aikens	Kansas City AL	2	1980
Willie Aikens	Kansas City AL	2	1980
Willie McGee	St. Louis NL	2*	1982
Eddie Murray	Baltimore AL	2*	1983
Alan Trammell	Detroit AL	2*	1984
Kirk Gibson	Detroit AL	2	1984
Gary Carter	New York NL	2	1986

* Indicates consecutive home runs.

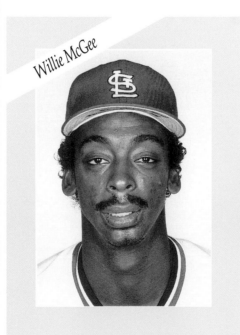

Willie McGee

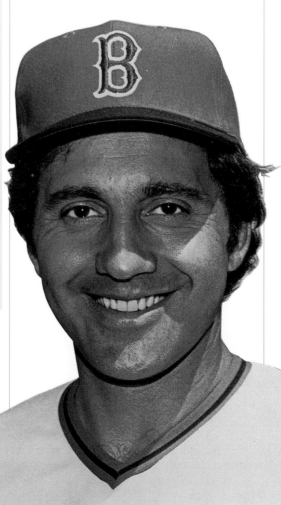

RIGHT: *Rico Petrocelli*

Most Complete Games Pitched in a World Series

T o have been able to make the list of the most complete games pitched in a World Series, a player usually had to be considered the ace of the staff. Selected by the manager to pitch the decisive first game, the pitcher was then called upon to hurl either a pivotal middle game or the crucial final game. In most of these cases they pitched on very few days rest, realizing that a loss could cost the team the Series.

In a four-game Series, one of the record-holders is Sandy Koufax, who pitched two complete games for the 1963 Los Angeles Dodgers. Among the players in a seven-game Series who pitched three complete games are Mickey Lolich, Lew Burdette, Walter Johnson, and Bob Gibson. Gibson was such an integral part of the St. Louis rotation that he won three games in the 1967 Series and then repeated the effort in 1968!

MOST COMPLETE GAMES PITCHED IN A WORLD SERIES

PITCHER	TEAM	GAMES	PITCHED	YEAR
Dick Rudolph	Boston NL	4	2	1914
Waite Hoyt	New York AL	4	2	1928
Red Ruffing	New York AL	4	2	1938
Sandy Koufax	Los Angeles NL	4	2	1963
Christy Mathewson	New York NL	5	3	1905
Jack Coombs	Philadelphia AL	5	3	1910
Chief Bender	Philadelphia AL	6	3	1911
Hippo Vaughn	Chicago NL	6	3	1918
Babe Adams	Pittsburgh NL	7	3	1909
George Mullin	Detroit AL	7	3	1909
Stan Coveleski	Cleveland AL	7	3	1920
Walter Johnson	Washington AL	7	3	1925
Bobo Newsom	Detroit AL	7	3	1940
Lew Burdette	Milwaukee NL	7	3	1957
Bob Gibson	St. Louis NL	7	3	1967
Bob Gibson	St. Louis NL	7	3	1968
Mickey Lolich	Detroit AL	7	3	1968

Sandy Koufax

LEFT: *Lew Burdette*   **RIGHT:** *Bob Gibson*

Pitchers with Four World Series Victories

A s in so many other of the Series categories, it helped to be a Yankee. Having won more championships than any other team, the New York Yankees are adequately represented on World Series' record lists. Pitching victories is no exception!

Leading the hurler brigade is Whitey Ford, who carved 10 victory notches in his belt. Following Ford are Allie Reynolds, Red Ruffing, and Bob Gibson of the St. Louis Cardinals. Gibson was able to record his seven wins in only three World Series.

Among the other more successful Series pitchers are Lefty Gomez, Catfish Hunter, Sandy Koufax, and Ken Holtzman.

RIGHT: *Chief Bender*

Allie Reynolds

PITCHERS WITH FOUR OR MORE WORLD SERIES VICTORIES

PITCHER AND CLUB	YEARS	WINS	LOSSES
Whitey Ford, New York AL	11	10	8
Red Ruffing, New York AL	7	7	2
Allie Reynolds, New York AL	6	7	2
Bob Gibson, St. Louis NL	3	7	2
Lefty Gomez, New York AL	4	6	0
Chief Bender, Philadelphia AL	5	6	4
Waite Hoyt, New York–Philadelphia AL	6	6	4
Jack Coombs, Philadelphia AL–Brooklyn NL	3	5	0
Herb Pennock, New York AL	3	5	0
Vic Raschi, New York AL	5	5	3
Catfish Hunter, Oakland–New York AL	6	5	3
Three-Finger Brown, Chicago NL	4	5	4
Christy Mathewson, New York NL	4	5	5
Monte Pearson, New York AL	4	4	0
Tommy Bridges, Detroit AL	3	4	1
Harry Brecheen, St. Louis NL	3	4	1
Ed Lopat, New York AL	4	4	1
Johnny Podres, Brooklyn–Los Angeles NL	4	4	1
Ken Holtzman, Oakland AL	3	4	1
Lefty Grove, Philadelphia AL	2	4	2
Carl Hubbell, New York NL	3	4	2
Lew Burdette, Milwaukee NL	2	4	2
Don Larsen, New York AL–San Francisco NL	5	4	2
Dave McNally, Baltimore AL	4	4	2
Jim Palmer, Baltimore AL	6	4	2
Sandy Koufax, Los Angeles NL	4	4	3
George Earnshaw, Philadelphia AL	3	4	3
Warren Spahn, Boston NL–Milwaukee NL	3	4	3
Bob Turley, New York AL	5	4	3
Art Nehf, New York NL	4	4	4

LEFT: *Whitey Ford had a lifetime record of ten wins and eight losses in World Series play.*

Lowest Earned-Run Average in a World Series, 14 or More Innings

S ince a pitcher's goal is to shut down the opposition, it means perfection when he doesn't allow the other team to score a run. In the history of the World Series, a few pitchers have shut down the enemy while still hurling much more than a token few innings.

Those who have compiled an earned-run average of 0.00 in a World Series include Christy Mathewson, Carl Hubbell, and Waite Hoyt.

Whitey Ford, who could perhaps be considered the best World Series pitcher ever, twice compiled a 0.00 ERA while tossing the ball for the New York Yankees in 1960 and 1961.

LOWEST EARNED-RUN AVERAGE IN A WORLD SERIES, 14 OR MORE INNINGS

PITCHER	TEAM	ERA	INNINGS	YEAR
Christy Mathewson	New York NL	0.00	27	1905
Waite Hoyt	New York AL	0.00	27	1921
Carl Hubbell	New York NL	0.00	20	1933
Whitey Ford	New York AL	0.00	18	1960
Joe McGinnity	New York NL	0.00	17	1905
Duster Mails	Cleveland AL	0.00	15⅔	1920
Rube Benton	New York NL	0.00	14	1917
Whitey Ford	New York AL	0.00	14	1961

BELOW: Waite Hoyt

ABOVE: Carl Hubbell

Most Saves in a World Series (Since 1969)

S ince the save became an official statistic in 1969, some bullpen stoppers have had the chance to show their mettle in the World Series. With the game on the line, these aces came to the mound and successfully put out the fire.

Kent Tekulve of the 1979 Pittsburgh Pirates holds the record with three saves in a seven-game World Series. The other relievers all compiled two saves in Series of varying lengths.

Pitchers like Goose Gossage, Willie Hernandez, and Tug McGraw all hurled their way into World Series history by mowing down the opposition when the game was on the line.

MOST SAVES IN A WORLD SERIES (SINCE 1969)

PITCHER	TEAM	GAMES	SAVES	YEAR
Will McEnaney	Cincinnati NL	4	2	1976
Rollie Fingers	Oakland AL	5	2	1974
Tippy Martinez	Baltimore AL	5	2	1983
Willie Hernandez	Detroit AL	5	2	1984
Tug McGraw	Philadelphia NL	6	2	1980
Goose Gossage	New York AL	6	2	1981
Kent Tekulve	Pittsburgh NL	7	3	1979

LEFT: Kent Tekulve holds the record for most saves in a World Series, with three saves in the seven-game 1979 Series.

Most Stolen Bases in a World Series

T hose players blessed with swift feet don't necessarily make it to the World Series. But if their team battles into the Fall Classic, some of the game's speedsters have had a chance to show their stuff.

For example, stolen-base expert Lou Brock set the record for swipes in a seven-game Series by stealing seven bases in the 1967 World Series. Then the following year Brock duplicated the mark!

On the other side of the coin, the four-game minimum Series, four players share the record of two stolen bases. Joining old-timers Charlie Deal and Walter "Rabbit" Maranville are the more contemporary Cesar Geronimo and Joe Morgan.

MOST STOLEN BASES IN A WORLD SERIES

PLAYER	TEAM	GAMES	STEALS	YEAR
Charlie Deal	Boston NL	4	2	1914
Rabbit Maranville	Boston NL	4	2	1914
Cesar Geronimo	Cincinnati NL	4	2	1976
Joe Morgan	Cincinnati NL	4	2	1976
Jimmy Slagle	Chicago NL	5	6	1907
Davy Lopes	Los Angeles NL	6	4	1981
Lou Brock	St. Louis NL	7	7	1967
Lou Brock	St. Louis NL	7	7	1968

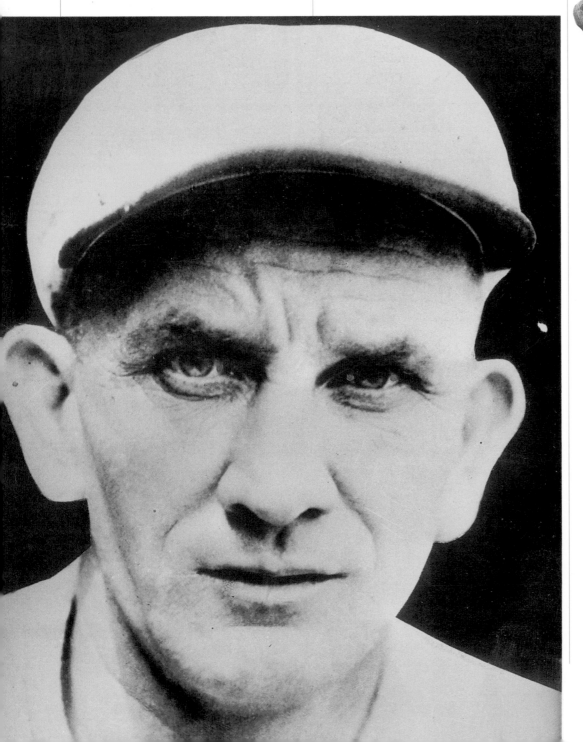

Rabbit Maranville stole two bases in the four-game 1914 World Series.

Lou Brock twice stole seven bases in a seven-game World Series!

Most Consecutive World Series Played

Very few teams get to play in consecutive World Series. But one of the greatest dynasties in the history of sports, the New York Yankees, used to make it a habit of playing in the Fall Classic. Therefore, it should come as no surprise that of the 17 men who share the honor of having played in five consecutive World Series, every one of them wore the Yankee pinstripes!

The list includes a veritable who's who in baseball history. Players such as Mickey Mantle, Yogi Berra, Roger Maris, Whitey Ford, Bobby Richardson, Phil Rizzuto, Hank Bauer, and Clete Boyer all competed in five consecutive World Series.

MOST CONSECUTIVE WORLD SERIES PLAYED

PLAYER	YEARS
Hank Bauer	1949–1953
Yogi Berra	1949–1953
Eddie Lopat	1949–1953
Johnny Mize	1949–1953
Vic Raschi	1949–1953
Allie Reynolds	1949–1953
Phil Rizzuto	1949–1953
Gene Woodling	1949–1953
Johnny Blanchard	1960–1964
Clete Boyer	1960–1964
Ralph Terry	1960–1964
Whitey Ford	1960–1964
Elston Howard	1960–1964
Hector Lopez	1960–1964
Mickey Mantle	1960–1964
Roger Maris	1960–1964
Bobby Richardson	1960–1964

Elston Howard

LEFT: Yogi Berra

BELOW: Bob Richardson

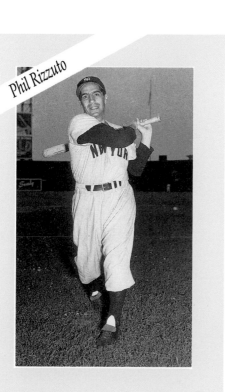

Phil Rizzuto

Most Valuable Player

In the crazy world of baseball statistics perhaps the biggest thrill of all is being named the league's Most Valuable Player. To be selected for this distinguished award by the Baseball Writers Association of America indicates that a player has contributed significantly to his victorious team. In 1931, when BBWAA began selecting the winners, Frankie Frisch won the award in the National League and Lefty Grove took the prize in the American League.

The only player to have won the award in both leagues is Frank Robinson. Robinson copped the award in 1961 with the National League's Cincinnati Reds and again in 1966 with the American League's Baltimore Orioles.

For years the argument has raged that the MVP should be reserved for everyday ballplayers, with pitchers relegated to the Cy Young. Regardless, a number of hurlers have won the MVP. Vida Blue, Sandy Koufax, Bob Gibson, and Don Newcombe have all had MVP seasons. Two relief pitchers, Rollie Fingers and Willie Hernandez, had such superior years coming in from the bullpen that they won both the Cy Young *and* the Most Valuable Player awards!

LEFT: Mike Schmidt

RIGHT: Steve Garvey

MOST VALUABLE PLAYER
AMERICAN LEAGUE

YEAR	PLAYER
1931	Lefty Grove, Philadelphia (P)
1932	Jimmy Foxx, Philadelphia (1B)
1933	Jimmy Foxx, Philadelphia (1B)
1934	Mickey Cochrane, Detroit (C)
1935	Hank Greenberg, Detroit (1B)
1936	Lou Gehrig, New York (1B)
1937	Charlie Gehringer, Detroit (2B)
1938	Jimmy Foxx, Boston (1B)
1939	Joe DiMaggio, New York (OF)
1940	Hank Greenberg, Detroit (1B)
1941	Joe DiMaggio, New York (OF)
1942	Joe Gordon, New York (2B)
1943	Spud Chandler, New York (P)
1944	Hal Newhouser, Detroit (P)
1945	Hal Newhouser, Detroit (P)
1946	Ted Williams, Boston (OF)
1947	Joe DiMaggio, New York (OF)
1948	Lou Boudreau, Cleveland (SS)
1949	Ted Williams, Boston (OF)
1950	Phil Rizzuto, New York (SS)
1951	Yogi Berra, New York (C)
1952	Bobby Shantz, Philadelphia (P)
1953	Al Rosen, Cleveland (3B)
1954	Yogi Berra, New York (C)
1955	Yogi Berra, New York (C)
1956	Mickey Mantle, New York (OF)
1957	Mickey Mantle, New York (OF)
1958	Jackie Jensen, Boston (OF)
1959	Nellie Fox, Chicago (2B)
1960	Roger Maris, New York (OF)
1961	Roger Maris, New York (OF)
1962	Mickey Mantle, New York (OF)
1963	Elston Howard, New York (C)
1964	Brooks Robinson, Baltimore (3B)
1965	Zoilo Versalles, Minnesota (SS)
1966	Frank Robinson, Baltimore (OF)
1967	Carl Yastrzemski, Boston (OF)
1968	Denny McLain, Detroit (P)
1969	Harmon Killebrew, Minnesota (3B)
1970	Boog Powell, Baltimore (1B)
1971	Vida Blue, Oakland (P)
1972	Richie Allen, Chicago (B)
1973	Reggie Jackson, Oakland (OF)
1974	Jeff Burroughs, Texas (OF)
1975	Fred Lynn, Boston (OF)
1976	Thurman Munson, New York (C)
1977	Rod Carew, Minnesota (1B)
1978	Jim Rice, Boston (OF)
1979	Don Baylor, California (DH)
1980	George Brett, Kansas City (3B)
1981	Rollie Fingers, Milwaukee (P)
1982	Robin Yount, Milwaukee (SS)
1983	Cal Ripken, Baltimore (SS)
1984	Willie Hernandez, Detroit (P)
1985	Don Mattingly, New York (1B)
1986	Roger Clemens, Boston (P)

NATIONAL LEAGUE

YEAR	PLAYER
1931	Frankie Frisch, St. Louis (2B)
1932	Chuck Klein, Philadelphia (OF)
1933	Carl Hubbell, New York (P)
1934	Dizzy Dean, St. Louis (P)
1935	Gabby Hartnett, Chicago (C)
1936	Carl Hubbell, New York (P)
1937	Joe Medwick, St. Louis (OF)
1938	Ernie Lombardi, Cincinnati (C)
1939	Bucky Walters, Cincinnati (P)
1940	Frank McCormick, Cincinnati (1B)
1941	Dolph Camilli, Brooklyn (1B)
1942	Mort Cooper, St. Louis (P)
1943	Stan Musial, St. Louis (OF)
1944	Marty Marion, St. Louis (SS)
1945	Phil Cavarretta, Chicago (1B)
1946	Stan Musial, St. Louis (1B)
1947	Bob Elliott, Boston (3B)
1948	Stan Musial, St. Louis (OF)
1949	Jackie Robinson, Brooklyn (2B)
1950	Jim Konstanty, Philadelphia (P)
1951	Roy Campanella, Brooklyn (C)
1952	Hank Sauer, Chicago (OF)
1953	Roy Campanella, Brooklyn (C)
1954	Willie Mays, New York (OF)
1955	Roy Campanella, Brooklyn (C)
1956	Don Newcombe, Brooklyn (P)
1957	Henry Aaron, Milwaukee (OF)
1958	Ernie Banks, Chicago (SS)
1959	Ernie Banks, Chicago (SS)
1960	Dick Groat, Pittsburgh (SS)
1961	Frank Robinson, Cincinnati (OF)
1962	Maury Wills, Los Angeles (SS)
1963	Sandy Koufax, Los Angeles (P)
1964	Ken Boyer, St. Louis (3B)
1965	Willie Mays, San Francisco (OF)
1966	Roberto Clemente, Pittsburgh (OF)
1967	Orlando Cepeda, St. Louis (1B)
1968	Bob Gibson, St. Louis (P)
1969	Willie McCovey, San Francisco (1B)
1970	Johnny Bench, Cincinnati (C)
1971	Joe Torre, St. Louis (3B)
1972	Johnny Bench, Cincinnati (C)
1973	Pete Rose, Cincinnati (OF)
1974	Steve Garvey, Los Angeles (1B)
1975	Joe Morgan, Cincinnati (2B)
1976	Joe Morgan, Cincinnati (2B)
1977	George Foster, Cincinnati (OF)
1978	Dave Parker, Pittsburgh (OF)
1979	Keith Hernandez, St. Louis (1B)
1979	Willie Stargell, Pittsburgh (1B)
1980	Mike Schmidt, Philadelphia (3B)
1981	Mike Schmidt, Philadelphia (3B)
1982	Dale Murphy, Atlanta (OF)
1983	Dale Murphy, Atlanta (OF)
1984	Ryne Sandberg, Chicago (2B)
1985	Willie McGee, St. Louis (OF)
1986	Mike Schmidt, Philadelphia (3B)

George Brett

Ryne Sandberg

LEFT: *Joe DiMaggio*

Cy Young Award

Named after one of the greatest pitchers ever to take the mound, the Cy Young Award is given to the best hurlers of the year by the Baseball Writers Association. Prior to 1967, only one award was given. However, since 1966 the top American and National League pitchers get the recognition.

Many say that because Sandy Koufax won the award three times that the league division was created. Dandy Sandy took high honors in 1963, 1965, and 1966. In fact, Dodger's teammate Don Drysdale won it in 1962 and Dean Chance in 1964, so a good case was made to "break up the Dodgers."

In any event, some of the Cy Young winners have been Steve Carlton, Ron Guidry, Tom Seaver, Bob Gibson, and Catfish Hunter. In some cases a relief pitcher has cracked the list, proving that consistently putting out the fire earns some respect. Among the relievers to win the Cy Young Award are Sparky Lyle, Rollie Fingers, and Willie Hernandez.

1969	Tom Seaver, New York (RH)
1970	Bob Gibson, St. Louis (RH)
1971	Ferguson Jenkins, Chicago (RH)
1972	Steve Carlton, Philadelphia (LH)
1973	Tom Seaver, New York (RH)
1974	Mike Marshall, Los Angeles (RH)
1975	Tom Seaver, New York (RH)
1976	Randy Jones, San Diego (LH)
1977	Steve Carlton, Philadelphia (LH)
1978	Gaylord Perry, San Diego (RH)
1979	Bruce Sutter, Chicago (RH)
1980	Steve Carlton, Philadelphia (LH)
1981	Fernando Valenzuela, Los Angeles (LH)
1982	Steve Carlton, Philadelphia (LH)
1983	John Denny, Philadelphia (RH)
1984	Rick Sutcliffe, Chicago (RH)
1985	Dwight Gooden, New York (RH)
1986	Mike Scott, Houston (RH)

CY YOUNG AWARD
AMERICAN LEAGUE

YEAR	PLAYER
1958	Bob Turley, New York (RH)
1959	Early Wynn, Chicago (RH)
1961	Whitey Ford, New York (LH)
1964	Dean Chance, Los Angeles (RH)
1967	Jim Lonborg, Boston (RH)
1968	Denny McLain, Detroit (RH)
1969	Mike Cuellar, Baltimore (tie) (LH)
1969	Denny McLain, Detroit (tie) (RH)
1970	Jim Perry, Minnesota (RH)
1971	Vida Blue, Oakland (LH)
1972	Gaylord Perry, Cleveland (RH)
1973	Jim Palmer, Baltimore (RH)
1974	Jim (Catfish) Hunter, Oakland (RH)
1975	Jim Palmer, Baltimore (RH)
1976	Jim Palmer, Baltimore (RH)
1977	Sparky Lyle, New York (LH)
1978	Ron Guidry, New York (LH)
1979	Mike Flanagan, Baltimore (LH)
1980	Steve Stone, Baltimore (RH)
1981	Rollie Fingers, Milwaukee (RH)
1982	Pete Vuckovich, Milwaukee (RH)
1983	LaMarr Hoyt, Chicago (RH)
1984	Willie Hernandez, Detroit (LH)
1985	Bret Saberhagen, Kansas City (RH)
1986	Roger Clemens, Boston (RH)

NATIONAL LEAGUE

YEAR	PLAYER
1956	Don Newcombe, Brooklyn (RH)
1957	Warren Spahn, Milwaukee (LH)
1960	Vernon Law, Pittsburgh (RH)
1962	Don Drysdale, Los Angeles (RH)
1963	Sandy Koufax, Los Angeles (LH)
1965	Sandy Koufax, Los Angeles (LH)
1966	Sandy Koufax, Los Angeles (LH)
1967	Mike McCormick, San Francisco (LH)
1968	Bob Gibson, St. Louis (RH)

Bret Saberhagen

LEFT: *Rick Sutcliffe*

Mike Scott

LEFT: Don Drysdale

Waite Hoyt

ABOVE: Fernando Valenzuela

Rookie of the Year

S ome of the game's most memorable players had banner rookie years. Whether fooling veterans with their pitching or cracking the ball with consistency, these players were able to garner the coveted Rookie of the Year Award. The award, presented annually by the Baseball Writers Association of America, came into being in 1947. The first winner was Jackie Robinson of the Brooklyn Dodgers. In 1948, Al Dark won the award while playing for the Boston Braves.

In 1949 separate league selection began with Don Newcombe of the Brooklyn Dodgers and Roy Sievers of the St. Louis Browns winning the award. Others who have been selected as Rookie of the Year include Pete Rose, Fernando Valenzuela, Cal Ripken, Eddie Murray, Willie Mays, Carlton Fisk, and Dwight Gooden.

BELOW: Steve Sax

ROOKIE OF THE YEAR
AMERICAN LEAGUE

YEAR	PLAYER
1949	Roy Sievers, St. Louis (OF)
1950	Walt Dropo, Boston (1B)
1951	Gil McDougald, New York (3B)
1952	Harry Byrd, Philadelphia (P)
1953	Harvey Kuenn, Detroit (SS)
1954	Bob Grim, New York (P)
1955	Herb Score, Cleveland (P)
1956	Luis Aparicio, Chicago (SS)
1957	Tony Kubek, New York (SS)
1958	Albie Pearson, Washington (OF)
1959	Bob Allison, Washington (OF)
1960	Ron Hansen, Baltimore (SS)
1961	Don Schwall, Boston (P)
1962	Tom Tresh, New York (SS)
1963	Gary Peters, Chicago (P)
1964	Tony Oliva, Minnesota (OF)
1965	Curt Blefary, Baltimore (OF)
1966	Tommie Agee, Chicago (OF)
1967	Rod Carew, Minnesota (2B)
1968	Stan Bahnsen, New York (P)
1969	Lou Piniella, Kansas City (OF)
1970	Thurman Munson, New York (C)
1971	Chris Chambliss, Cleveland (1B)
1972	Carlton Fisk, Boston (C)
1973	Al Bumbry, Baltimore (OF)
1974	Mike Hargrove, Texas (1B)
1975	Fred Lynn, Boston (OF)
1976	Mark Fidrych, Detroit (P)
1977	Eddie Murray, Baltimore (DH)
1978	Lou Whitaker, Detroit (2B)
1979	Alfredo Griffin, Toronto (SS)
1979	John Castino, Minnesota (3B)
1980	Joe Charboneau, Cleveland (OF)
1981	Dave Righetti, New York (P)
1982	Cal Ripken, Jr., Baltimore (SS)
1983	Ron Kittle, Chicago (OF)
1984	Alvin Davis, Seattle (1B)
1985	Ozzie Guillen, Chicago (SS)
1986	José Canseco, Oakland (OF)
1987	Mark McGwire, Oakland (OF)

NATIONAL LEAGUE

YEAR	PLAYER
1947	Jackie Robinson, Brooklyn (1B)
1948	Alvin Dark, Boston (SS)
1949	Don Newcombe, Brooklyn (P)
1950	Sam Jethroe, Boston (OF)
1951	Willie Mays, New York (OF)
1952	Joe Black, Brooklyn (P)
1953	Junior Gilliam, Brooklyn (2B)
1954	Wally Moon, St. Louis (OF)
1955	Bill Virdon, St. Louis (OF)
1956	Frank Robinson, Cincinnati (OF)
1957	Jack Sanford, Philadelphia (P)
1958	Orlando Cepeda, San Francisco (1B)
1959	Willie McCovey, San Francisco (1B)
1960	Frank Howard, Los Angeles (OF)
1961	Billy Williams, Chicago (OF)
1962	Ken Hubbs, Chicago (2B)
1963	Pete Rose, Cincinnati (2B)
1964	Richie Allen, Philadelphia (3B)
1965	Jim Lefebvre, Los Angeles (2B)
1966	Tommy Helms, Cincinnati (2B)
1967	Tom Seaver, New York (P)
1968	Johnny Bench, Cincinnati (C)
1969	Ted Sizemore, Los Angeles (2B)
1970	Carl Morton, Montreal (P)
1971	Earl Williams, Atlanta (C)
1972	Jon Matlack, New York (P)

1973	Gary Matthews, San Francisco (OF)
1974	Bake McBride, St. Louis (OF)
1975	John Montefusco, San Francisco (P)
1976	Pat Zachry, Cincinnati (P)
1976	Butch Metzger, San Diego (P)
1977	Andre Dawson, Montreal (OF)
1978	Bob Horner, Atlanta (3B)
1979	Rick Sutcliffe, Los Angeles (P)
1980	Steve Howe, Los Angeles (P)
1981	Fernando Valenzuela, Los Angeles (P)
1982	Steve Sax, Los Angeles (2B)
1983	Darryl Strawberry, New York (OF)
1984	Dwight Gooden, New York (P)
1985	Vince Coleman, St. Louis (OF)
1986	Robby Thompson, San Francisco (2B)
1987	Benito Santiago, San Diego (C)

Andre Dawson

Robby Thompson

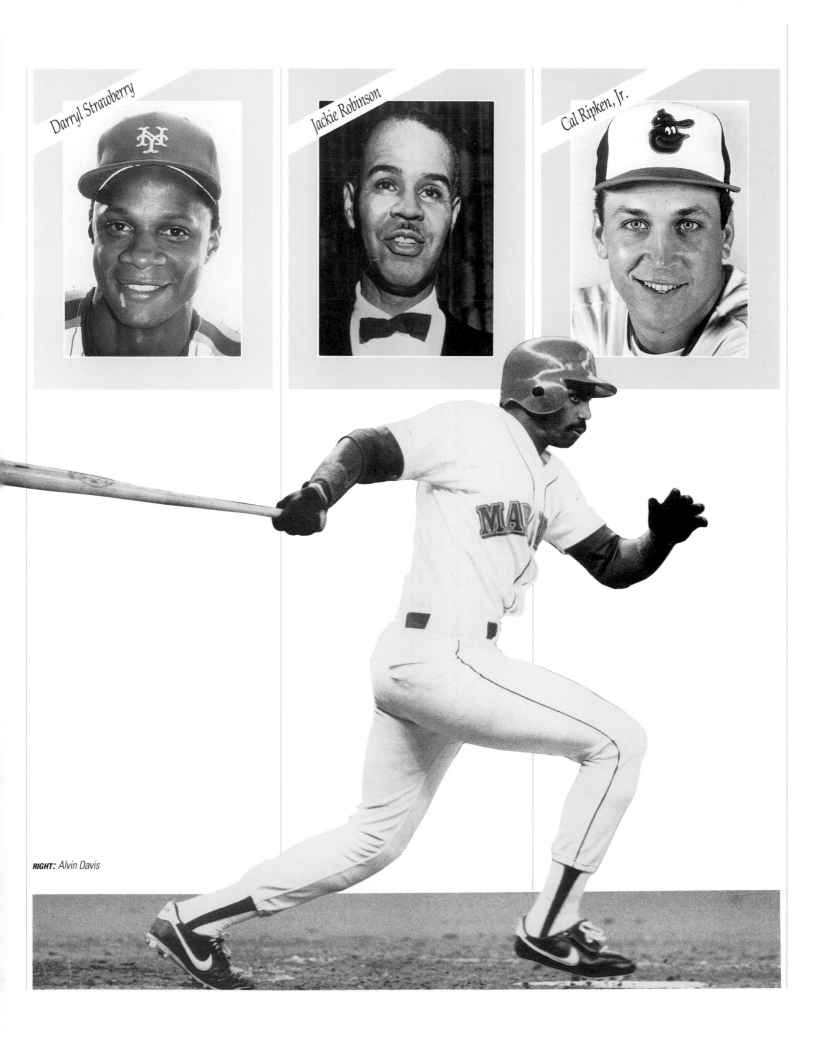

Darryl Strawberry

Jackie Robinson

Cal Ripken, Jr.

RIGHT: *Alvin Davis*

Rawlings Gold Glove Award

The Rawlings Gold Glove Award®, symbolic of fielding excellence, is the only award bestowed upon the game's greatest glovemen. Established in 1957, the first team consisted of infielders Gil Hodges, Roy McMillan, Nellie Fox, and Frank Malzone. The premier fielding outfielders were Willie Mays, Al Kaline, and Minnie Minoso. Joining the team was pitcher Bobby Shantz and catcher Sherm Lollar.

Since 1958 the Gold Glove has been presented annually to 18 players, nine in each league, by position. These superior ballplayers are voted and selected as the best-fielding players at their respective position by coaches and managers in each league prior to the conclusion of the regular baseball season.

Looking at the list of past winners yields a who's who of the baseball world. Players such as Dave Winfield, Willie McGee, George Brett, Jesse Barfield, and Mike Schmidt all earned their Gold Glove with outstanding play on the field.

BELOW: Frank White

ABOVE: Del Crandall and Henry Aaron receive the first National League Rawlings Gold Glove Award (1958).

RAWLINGS GOLD GLOVE AWARD® TEAMS

1957 MAJORS

P	Bobby Shantz, New York AL
C	Mickey Lollar, Chicago AL
1B	Gil Hodges, Brooklyn
2B	Nellie Fox, Chicago AL
3B	Frank Malzone, Boston
SS	Roy McMillan, Cincinnati
LF	Minnie Minoso, Chicago AL
CF	Willie Mays, New York, NL
RF	Al Kaline, Detroit

1958 AMERICAN

P	Bobby Shantz, New York
C	Mickey Lollar, Chicago
1B	Vic Power, Cleveland
2B	Frank Bolling, Detroit
3B	Frank Malzone, Boston
SS	Luis Aparicio, Chicago
LF	Norm Siebern, New York
CF	Jimmy Piersall, Boston
RF	Al Kaline, Detroit

1958 NATIONAL

P	Harvey Haddix, Cincinnati
C	Del Crandall, Milwaukee
1B	Gil Hodges, Los Angeles
2B	Bill Mazeroski, Pittsburgh
3B	Clete Boyer, St. Louis
SS	Roy McMillan, Cincinnati
LF	Frank Robinson, Cincinnati
CF	Willie Mays, San Francisco
RF	Henry Aaron, Milwaukee

1959 AMERICAN

P	Bobby Shantz, New York
C	Mickey Lollar, Chicago
1B	Vic Power, Cleveland
2B	Nellie Fox, Chicago
3B	Frank Malzone, Boston
SS	Luis Aparicio, Chicago
LF	Minnie Minoso, Cleveland
CF	Al Kaline, Detroit
RF	Jackie Jensen, Boston

1959 NATIONAL

P	Harvey Haddix, Pittsburgh
C	Del Crandall, Milwaukee
1B	Gil Hodges, Los Angeles
2B	Charlie Neal, Los Angeles
3B	Clete Boyer, St. Louis
SS	Roy McMillan, Cincinnati
LF	Jackie Brandt, St. Louis
CF	Willie Mays, San Francisco
RF	Henry Aaron, Milwaukee

1960 AMERICAN

P	Bobby Shantz, New York
C	Earl Battey, Washington
1B	Vic Power, Cleveland
2B	Nellie Fox, Chicago
3B	Brooks Robinson, Baltimore
SS	Luis Aparicio, Chicago
LF	Minnie Minoso, Chicago
CF	Jim Landis, Chicago
RF	Roger Maris, New York

1960 NATIONAL

P	Harvey Haddix, Pittsburgh
C	Del Crandall, Milwaukee
1B	Bill White, St. Louis
2B	Bill Mazeroski, Pittsburgh
3B	Clete Boyer, St. Louis
SS	Ernie Banks, Chicago
LF	Wally Moon, Los Angeles
CF	Willie Mays, San Francisco
RF	Henry Aaron, Milwaukee

1961 AMERICAN

P	Lyn Lary, Detroit
C	Earl Battey, Chicago
1B	Vic Power, Cleveland
2B	Bobby Richardson, New York
3B	Brooks Robinson, Baltimore
SS	Luis Aparicio, Chicago
OF	Al Kaline, Detroit
OF	Jimmy Piersall, Cleveland
OF	Jim Landis, Chicago

1961 NATIONAL

P	Bobby Shantz, Pittsburgh
C	Johnny Roseboro, Los Angeles
1B	Bill White, St. Louis
2B	Bill Mazeroski, Pittsburgh
3B	Clete Boyer, St. Louis
SS	Maury Wills, Los Angeles
OF	Willie Mays, San Francisco
OF	Roberto Clemente, Pittsburgh
OF	Vada Pinson, Cincinnati

1962 AMERICAN

P	Jim Kaat, Minnesota
C	Earl Battey, Minnesota
1B	Vic Power, Minnesota
2B	Bobby Richardson, New York
3B	Brooks Robinson, Baltimore
SS	Luis Aparicio, Chicago
OF	Jim Landis, Chicago
OF	Mickey Mantle, New York
OF	Al Kaline, Detroit

1962 NATIONAL

P	Bobby Shantz, St. Louis
C	Del Crandall, Milwaukee
1B	Bill White, St. Louis
2B	Ken Hubbs, Chicago
3B	Jim Davenport, San Francisco
SS	Maury Wills, Los Angeles
OF	Willie Mays, San Francisco
OF	Roberto Clemente, Pittsburgh
OF	Bill Virdon, Pittsburgh

1963 AMERICAN

P	Jim Kaat, Minnesota
C	Elston Howard, New York
1B	Vic Power, Minnesota
2B	Bobby Richardson, New York
3B	Brooks Robinson, Baltimore
SS	Zoilo Versalles, Minnesota
OF	Al Kaline, Detroit
OF	Carl Yastrzemski, Boston
OF	Jim Landis, Chicago

1963 NATIONAL

P	Bobby Shantz, St. Louis
C	Johnny Edwards, Cincinnati
1B	Bill White, St. Louis
2B	Bill Mazeroski, Pittsburgh
3B	Clete Boyer, St. Louis
SS	Bobby Wine, Philadelphia

BELOW: *Gary Pettis*

OF	Willie Mays, San Francisco
OF	Roberto Clemente, Pittsburgh
OF	Curt Flood, St. Louis

1964 AMERICAN

P	Jim Kaat, Minnesota
C	Elston Howard, New York
1B	Vic Power, Los Angeles
2B	Bobby Richardson, New York
3B	Brooks Robinson, Baltimore
SS	Luis Aparicio, Baltimore
OF	Al Kaline, Detroit
OF	Jim Landis, Chicago
OF	Vic Davalillo, Cleveland

1964 NATIONAL

P	Bobby Shantz, Philadelphia
C	Johnny Edwards, Cincinnati
1B	Bill White, St. Louis
2B	Bill Mazeroski, Pittsburgh
3B	Ron Santo, Chicago
SS	Ruben Amaro, Philadelphia
OF	Willie Mays, San Francisco
OF	Roberto Clemente, Pittsburgh
OF	Curt Flood, St. Louis

1965 AMERICAN

P	Jim Kaat, Minnesota
C	Bill Freehan, Detroit
1B	Joe Pepitone, New York
2B	Bobby Richardson, New York
3B	Brooks Robinson, Baltimore
SS	Zoilo Versalles, Minnesota
OF	Al Kaline, Detroit
OF	Tom Tresh, New York
OF	Carl Yastrzemski, Boston

1965 NATIONAL

P	Bob Gibson, St. Louis
C	Joe Torre, Atlanta
1B	Bill White, St. Louis
2B	Bill Mazeroski, Pittsburgh
3B	Ron Santo, Chicago
SS	Leo Cardenas, Cincinnati
OF	Willie Mays, San Francisco
OF	Roberto Clemente, Pittsburgh
OF	Curt Flood, St. Louis

1966 AMERICAN

P	Jim Kaat, Minnesota
C	Bill Freehan, Detroit
1B	Joe Pepitone, New York
2B	Bobby Knoop, California
3B	Brooks Robinson, Baltimore
SS	Luis Aparicio, Baltimore
OF	Al Kaline, Detroit
OF	Tommy Agee, Chicago
OF	Tony Oliva, Minnesota

1966 NATIONAL

P	Bob Gibson, St. Louis
C	Johnny Roseboro, Los Angeles
1B	Bill White, Philadelphia
2B	Bill Mazeroski, Pittsburgh
3B	Ron Santo, Chicago
SS	Gene Alley, Pittsburgh
OF	Willie Mays, San Francisco
OF	Curt Flood, St. Louis
OF	Roberto Clemente, Pittsburgh

1967 AMERICAN

P	Jim Kaat, Minnesota
C	Bill Freehan, Detroit
1B	George Scott, Boston
2B	Bobby Knoop, California
3B	Brooks Robinson, Baltimore
SS	Jim Fregosi, California
OF	Carl Yastrzemski, Boston
OF	Paul Blair, Baltimore
OF	Al Kaline, Detroit

Gary Gaetti

1967 NATIONAL

P	Bob Gibson, St. Louis
C	Randy Hundley, Chicago
1B	Wes Parker, Los Angeles
2B	Bill Mazeroski, Pittsburgh
3B	Ron Santo, Chicago
SS	Gene Alley, Pittsburgh
OF	Roberto Clemente, Pittsburgh
OF	Curt Flood, St. Louis
OF	Willie Mays, San Francisco

1968 AMERICAN

P	Jim Kaat, Minnesota
C	Bill Freehan, Detroit
1B	George Scott, Boston
2B	Bobby Knoop, California
3B	Brooks Robinson, Baltimore
SS	Luis Aparicio, Chicago
OF	Mickey Stanley, Detroit
OF	Carl Yastrzemski, Boston
OF	Reggie Smith, Boston

1968 NATIONAL

P	Bob Gibson, St. Louis
C	Johnny Bench, Cincinnati
1B	Wes Parker, Los Angeles
2B	Glenn Beckert, Chicago
3B	Ron Santo, Chicago
SS	Dal Maxvill, St. Louis
OF	Willie Mays, San Francisco
OF	Roberto Clemente, Pittsburgh
OF	Curt Flood, St. Louis

1969 AMERICAN

P	Jim Kaat, Minnesota
C	Bill Freehan, Detroit
1B	Joe Pepitone, New York
2B	Davy Johnson, Baltimore
3B	Brooks Robinson, Baltimore
SS	Mark Belanger, Baltimore
OF	Paul Blair, Baltimore
OF	Mickey Stanley, Detroit
OF	Carl Yastrzemski, Boston

1969 NATIONAL

P	Bob Gibson, St. Louis
C	Johnny Bench, Cincinnati
1B	Wes Parker, Los Angeles

2B	Felix Millan, Atlanta
3B	Clete Boyer, Atlanta
SS	Don Kessinger, Chicago
OF	Roberto Clemente, Pittsburgh
OF	Curt Flood, St. Louis
OF	Pete Rose, Cincinnati

1970 AMERICAN

P	Jim Kaat, Minnesota
C	Ray Fosse, Cleveland
1B	Jim Spencer, California
2B	Davy Johnson, Baltimore
3B	Brooks Robinson, Baltimore
SS	Luis Aparicio, Chicago
OF	Mickey Stanley, Detroit
OF	Paul Blair, Baltimore
OF	Ken Berry, Chicago

1970 NATIONAL

P	Bob Gibson, St. Louis
C	Johnny Bench, Cincinnati
1B	Wes Parker, Los Angeles
2B	Tommy Helms, Cincinnati
3B	Doug Rader, Houston
SS	Don Kessinger, Chicago
OF	Roberto Clemente, Pittsburgh
OF	Tommy Agee, New York
OF	Pete Rose, Cincinnati

1971 AMERICAN

P	Jim Kaat, Minnesota
C	Ray Fosse, Cleveland
1B	George Scott, Boston
2B	Davy Johnson, Baltimore
3B	Brooks Robinson, Baltimore
SS	Mark Belanger, Baltimore
OF	Paul Blair, Baltimore
OF	Amos Otis, Kansas City
OF	Carl Yastrzemski, Boston

1971 NATIONAL

P	Bob Gibson, St. Louis
C	Johnny Bench, Cincinnati
1B	Wes Parker, Los Angeles
2B	Tommy Helms, Cincinnati
3B	Doug Rader, Houston
SS	Bud Harrelson, New York
OF	Roberto Clemente, Pittsburgh
OF	Bobby Bonds, San Francisco
OF	Willie Davis, Los Angeles

1972 AMERICAN

P	Jim Kaat, Minnesota
C	Carlton Fisk, Boston
1B	George Scott, Milwaukee
2B	Doug Griffin, Boston
3B	Brooks Robinson, Baltimore
SS	Ed Brinkman, Detroit
OF	Paul Blair, Baltimore
OF	Bobby Murcer, New York
OF	Ken Berry, California

BELOW: Jesse Barfield

1972 NATIONAL

P	Bob Gibson, St. Louis
C	Johnny Bench, Cincinnati
1B	Wes Parker, Los Angeles
2B	Felix Millan, Atlanta
3B	Doug Rader, Houston
SS	Larry Bowa, Philadelphia
OF	Roberto Clemente, Pittsburgh
OF	Cesar Cedeno, Houston
OF	Willie Davis, Los Angeles

1973 AMERICAN

P	Jim Kaat, Chicago
C	Thurman Munson, New York
1B	George Scott, Milwaukee
2B	Bobby Grich, Baltimore
3B	Brooks Robinson, Baltimore
SS	Mark Belanger, Baltimore
OF	Paul Blair, Baltimore
OF	Amos Otis, Kansas City
OF	Mickey Stanley, Detroit

1973 NATIONAL

P	Bob Gibson, St. Louis
C	Johnny Bench, Cincinnati
1B	Mike Jorgensen, Montreal
2B	Joe Morgan, Cincinnati
3B	Doug Rader, Houston
SS	Roger Metzger, Houston
OF	Bobby Bonds, San Francisco
OF	Cesar Cedeno, Houston
OF	Willie Davis, Los Angeles

1974 AMERICAN

P	Jim Kaat, Chicago
C	Thurman Munson, New York
1B	George Scott, Milwaukee
2B	Bobby Grich, Baltimore
3B	Brooks Robinson, Baltimore
SS	Mark Belanger, Baltimore
OF	Paul Blair, Baltimore
OF	Amos Otis, Kansas City
OF	Joe Rudi, Oakland

1974 NATIONAL

P	Randy Messersmith, Los Angeles
C	Johnny Bench, Cincinnati
1B	Steve Garvey, Los Angeles
2B	Joe Morgan, Cincinnati
3B	Doug Rader, Houston
SS	Dave Concepcion, Cincinnati
OF	Cesar Cedeno, Houston
OF	Cesar Geronimo, Cincinnati
OF	Bobby Bonds, San Francisco

1975 AMERICAN

P	Jim Kaat, Chicago
C	Thurman Munson, New York
1B	George Scott, Milwaukee
2B	Bobby Grich, Baltimore
3B	Brooks Robinson, Baltimore
SS	Mark Belanger, Baltimore
OF	Paul Blair, Baltimore
OF	Joe Rudi, Oakland
OF	Fred Lynn, Boston

1975 NATIONAL

P	Randy Messersmith, Los Angeles
C	Johnny Bench, Cincinnati
1B	Steve Garvey, Los Angeles
2B	Joe Morgan, Cincinnati
3B	Ken Reitz, St. Louis
SS	Dave Concepcion, Cincinnati
OF	Cesar Cedeno, Houston
OF	Cesar Geronimo, Cincinnati
OF	Gary Maddox, Philadelphia

1976 AMERICAN

P	Jim Palmer, Baltimore
C	Jim Sundberg, Texas
1B	George Scott, Milwaukee

ABOVE: Ozzie Smith and Willie Smith get their Gold Gloves.

2B	Bobby Grich, Baltimore
3B	Aurelio Rodrigues, Detroit
SS	Mark Belanger, Baltimore
OF	Joe Rudi, Oakland
OF	Dwight Evans, Boston
OF	Rick Manning, Cleveland

1976 NATIONAL

P	Jim Kaat, Philadelphia
C	Johnny Bench, Cincinnati
1B	Steve Garvey, Los Angeles
2B	Joe Morgan, Cincinnati
3B	Mike Schmidt, Philadelphia
SS	Dave Concepcion, Cincinnati
OF	Cesar Cedeno, Houston
OF	Cesar Geronimo, Cincinnati
OF	Gary Maddox, Philadelphia

1977 AMERICAN

P	Jim Palmer, Baltimore
C	Jim Sundberg, Texas
1B	Jim Spencer, Chicago
2B	Frank White, Kansas City
3B	Graig Nettles, New York
SS	Mark Belanger, Baltimore
OF	Juan Beniquez, Texas
OF	Carl Yastrzemski, Boston
OF	Al Cowens, Kansas City

1977 NATIONAL

P	Jim Kaat, Philadelphia
C	Johnny Bench, Cincinnati
1B	Steve Garvey, Los Angeles
2B	Joe Morgan, Cincinnati
3B	Mike Schmidt, Philadelphia
SS	Dave Concepcion, Cincinnati
OF	Cesar Geronimo, Cincinnati
OF	Gary Maddox, Philadelphia
OF	Dave Parker, Pittsburgh

1978 AMERICAN

P	Jim Palmer, Baltimore
C	Jim Sundberg, Texas
1B	Chris Chambliss, New York
2B	Frank White, Kansas City
3B	Graig Nettles, New York
SS	Mark Belanger, Baltimore
OF	Fred Lynn, Boston
OF	Dwight Evans, Boston
OF	Rick Miller, California

1978 NATIONAL

P	Phil Niekro, Atlanta
C	Bob Boone, Philadelphia
1B	Keith Hernandez, St. Louis
2B	Davey Lopez, Los Angeles

3B	Mike Schmidt, Philadelphia
SS	Larry Bowa, Philadelphia
OF	Gary Maddox, Philadelphia
OF	Dave Parker, Pittsburgh
OF	Bobby Valentine, Montreal

1979 AMERICAN

P	Jim Palmer, Baltimore
C	Jim Sundberg, Texas
1B	Cecil Cooper, Milwaukee
2B	Frank White, Kansas City
3B	Buddy Bell, Texas
SS	Rick Burleson, Boston
OF	Dwight Evans, Boston
OF	Sixto Lezcano, Milwaukee
OF	Fred Lynn, Boston

1979 NATIONAL

P	Phil Niekro, Atlanta
C	Bob Boone, Philadelphia
1B	Keith Hernandez, St. Louis
2B	Manny Trillo, Philadelphia
3B	Mike Schmidt, Philadelphia
SS	Dave Concepcion, Cincinnati
OF	Gary Maddox, Philadelphia
OF	Dave Parker, Pittsburgh
OF	Dave Winfield, San Diego

1980 AMERICAN

P	Mike Norris, Oakland
C	Jim Sundberg, Texas
1B	Cecil Cooper, Milwaukee
2B	Frank White, Kansas City
3B	Buddy Bell, Texas
SS	Allan Trammell, Detroit
OF	Fred Lynn, Boston
OF	Dale Murphy, Oakland
OF	Willie Wilson, Kansas City

1980 NATIONAL

P	Phil Niekro, Atlanta
C	Gary Carter, Montreal
1B	Keith Hernandez, St. Louis
2B	Doug Flynn, New York
3B	Mike Schmidt, Philadelphia

BELOW: *Gold Glove winner Dale Murphy holds his trophy.*

SS	Ozzie Smith, San Diego
OF	Andre Dawson, Montreal
OF	Gary Maddox, Philadelphia
OF	Dave Winfield, San Diego

1981 AMERICAN

P	Mike Norris, Oakland
C	Jim Sundberg, Texas
1B	Mike Squires, Chicago
2B	Frank White, Kansas City
3B	Buddy Bell, Texas
SS	Allan Trammell, Detroit
OF	Dale Murphy, Oakland
OF	Dwight Evans, Boston
OF	Rickey Henderson, Oakland

1981 NATIONAL

P	Steve Carlton, Philadelphia
C	Gary Carter, Montreal
1B	Keith Hernandez, St. Louis
2B	Manny Trillo, Philadelphia
3B	Mike Schmidt, Philadelphia
SS	Ozzie Smith, San Diego
OF	Andre Dawson, Montreal
OF	Gary Maddox, Philadelphia
OF	Dusty Baker, Los Angeles

1982 AMERICAN

P	Ron Guidry, New York
C	Bob Boone, California
1B	Eddie Murray, Baltimore
2B	Frank White, Kansas City
3B	Buddy Bell, Texas
SS	Robin Yount, Milwaukee
OF	Dwight Evans, Boston
OF	Dave Winfield, New York
OF	Dale Murphy, Oakland

1982 NATIONAL

P	Phil Niekro, Atlanta
C	Gary Carter, Montreal
1B	Keith Hernandez, St. Louis
2B	Manny Trillo, Philadelphia
3B	Mike Schmidt, Philadelphia
SS	Ozzie Smith, St. Louis
OF	Andre Dawson, Montreal
OF	Dale Murphy, Atlanta
OF	Gary Maddox, Philadelphia

1983 AMERICAN

P	Ron Guidry, New York
C	Lance Parrish, Detroit
1B	Eddie Murray, Baltimore
2B	Lou Whitaker, Detroit
3B	Buddy Bell, Texas
SS	Allan Trammell, Detroit
OF	Dwight Evans, Boston
OF	Dave Winfield, New York
OF	Dale Murphy, Oakland

1983 NATIONAL

P	Phil Niekro, Atlanta
C	Tony Pena, Pittsburgh
1B	Keith Hernandez, St. Louis–New York
2B	Ryne Sandberg, Chicago
3B	Mike Schmidt, Philadelphia
SS	Ozzie Smith, St. Louis
OF	Andre Dawson, Montreal
OF	Dale Murphy, Atlanta
OF	Willie McGee, St. Louis

1984 AMERICAN

P	Ron Guidry, New York
C	Lance Parrish, Detroit
1B	Eddie Murray, Baltimore
2B	Lou Whitaker, Detroit
3B	Buddy Bell, Texas
SS	Allan Trammell, Detroit
OF	Dwight Evans, Boston
OF	Dave Winfield, New York
OF	Dale Murphy, Oakland

1984 NATIONAL

P	Joaquin Andujar, St. Louis
C	Tony Pena, Pittsburgh
1B	Keith Hernandez, New York
2B	Ryne Sandberg, Chicago
3B	Mike Schmidt, Philadelphia
SS	Ozzie Smith, St. Louis
OF	Dale Murphy, Atlanta
OF	Bob Dernier, Chicago
OF	Andre Dawson, Montreal

1985 AMERICAN

P	Ron Guidry, New York
C	Lance Parrish, Detroit
1B	Don Mattingly, New York
2B	Lou Whitaker, Detroit
3B	George Brett, Kansas City
SS	Al Griffin, Oakland
OF	Dave Winfield, New York
OF	Dwight Evans, Boston
OF	Gary Pettis, California
OF	Dwayne Murphy, Oakland

1985 NATIONAL

P	Rick Reuschel, Pittsburgh
C	Tony Pena, Pittsburgh
1B	Keith Hernandez, New York
2B	Ryne Sandberg, Chicago
3B	Tim Wallach, Montreal
SS	Ozzie Smith, St. Louis
OF	Dale Murphy, Atlanta
OF	Andre Dawson, Montreal
OF	Willie McGee, St. Louis

1986 AMERICAN

P	Ron Guidry, Yankees
C	Bob Boone, California
1B	Don Mattingly, New York
2B	Frank White, Kansas Royals
3B	Gary Gaetti, Minnesota
SS	Tony Fernandez, Toronto
OF	Gary Pettis, California
OF	Jesse Barfield, Toronto
OF	Kirby Puckett, Minnesota

1986 NATIONAL

P	Fernando Valenzuela, Los Angeles
C	Jody Davis, Chicago
1B	Keith Hernandez, New York
2B	Ryne Sandberg, Chicago
3B	Mike Schmidt, Philadelphia
SS	Ozzie Smith, St. Louis
OF	Tony Gwynn, San Diego
OF	Willie McGee, St. Louis
OF	Dale Murphy, Atlanta

BELOW: *Tony Gwynn shows off his Gold Glove.*

Baseball Hall of Fame

W hen the cheering stops and long after a player takes off his uniform for the last time, another dream begins to emerge. Perhaps the ultimate achievement for a baseball player is to be elected to the Baseball Hall of Fame. Located in the quiet, New York State community called Cooperstown, the Hall of Fame is the shrine of professional baseball.

Elected based on their remarkable careers, the bronze images of the game's greatest players stand side by side, to be admired by their fans. Great names of the past such as Babe Ruth, Ty Cobb, and Grover Cleveland Alexander are joined by such relative newcomers as Hank Aaron, Catfish Hunter, and Juan Marichal.

But the Hall of Fame is not only for players. Such managers as Casey Stengel, John McGraw, and Walter Aston also have their place, as do those such as Kenesaw Mountain Landis and Branch Rickey, chosen for their meritorious service to the game. Starting with the great Satchel Paige and Buck Leonard in 1972, players have also been elected on the basis of their careers in the Negro Leagues (designated by an asterisk on the list below).

Billy Williams

Roy Campanella

LEFT: Umpire Bill Klen

BASEBALL HALL OF FAME

PLAYER	POSITION	CAREER DATES	YEAR SELECTED
Henry Aaron	OF	1954–1976	1982
Grover Alexander	P	1911–1930	1938
Cap Anson	1B	1876–1897	1939
Luis Aparicio	SS	1956–1973	1984
Luke Appling	SS	1930–1950	1964
Earl Averill	OF	1929–1941	1975
J. Frank Baker	3B	1908–1922	1955
Dave Bancroft	SS	1915–1930	1971
Ernie Banks	SS–1B	1953–1971	1977
Jake Beckley	1B	1888–1907	1971
James Bell*	OF		1974

Chief Bender	P	1903–1925	1938
Yogi Berra	C	1946–1965	1971
Jim Bottomley	1B	1922–1937	1974
Lou Boudreau	SS	1938–1952	1970
Roger Bresnahan	C	1897–1915	1945
Lou Brock	OF	1961–1979	1985
Dan Brouthers	1B	1879–1904	1945
Mordecai Brown	P	1903–1916	1949
Jesse Burkett	OF	1890–1905	1946
Roy Campanella	C	1948–1957	1969
Max Carey	OF	1910–1929	1961
Frank Chance	1B	1898–1914	1946
Oscar Charleston*	OF		1976
Jack Chesbro	P	1899–1909	1946

RIGHT: *Gabby Hartnet*

Roy Dandridge*			1987
Dizzy Dean	P	1930–1947	1953
Ed Delahanty	OF	1888–1903	1945
Bill Dickey	C	1928–1946	1954
Martin DiHigo*	P		1977
Joe DiMaggio	OF	1936–1951	1955
Bobby Doerr	2B	1937–1951	1986
Don Drysdale	P	1956–1969	1984
Hugh Duffy	OF	1888–1906	1945
Johnny Evers	2B	1902–1929	1946
Buck Ewing	C	1880–1897	1946
Red Faber	P	1914–1933	1964
Bob Feller	P	1936–1956	1962
Rick Ferrell	C	1929–1947	1984
Elmer Flick	OF	1898–1910	1963
Whitey Ford	P	1950–1967	1974
Jimmy Foxx	1B	1925–1945	1951
Frankie Frisch	2B	1919–1937	1947
Pud Galvin	P	1879–1892	1965
Lou Gehrig	1B	1923–1939	1939
Charlie Gehringer	2B	1924–1942	1949
Bob Gibson	P	1959–1975	1981
Josh Gibson*	C		1972
Lefty Gomez	P	1930–1943	1972
Goose Goslin	OF	1921–1938	1968
Hank Greenberg	1B	1930–1947	1956
Burleigh Grimes	P	1916–1934	1964
Lefty Grove	P	1925–1941	1947
Chick Hafey	OF	1924–1937	1971
Jesse Haines	P	1918–1937	1970
Billy Hamilton	OF	1888–1901	1961
Gabby Hartnett	C	1922–1941	1955
Harry Heilmann	OF	1914–1932	1952
Billy Herman	2B	1931–1947	1975

Pie Traynor

Fred Clarke	OF	1894–1915	1945
John Clarkson	P	1882–1894	1963
Roberto Clemente	OF	1955–1972	1973
Ty Cobb	OF	1905–1928	1936
Mickey Cochrane	C	1925–1937	1947
Eddie Collins	2B	1906–1930	1939
Jimmy Collins	3B	1895–1908	1945
Earle Combs	OF	1924–1935	1970
Roger Connor	1B	1880–1897	1976
Stan Coveleski	P	1912–1928	1969
Sam Crawford	OF	1899–1917	1957
Joe Cronin	SS	1926–1945	1956
Candy Cummings	P	1872–1877	1939
Kiki Cuyler	OF	1921–1938	1968

LEFT: *Baseball Commissioner Kennesaw Mountain Landis.*

LEFT: *Harry Hooper*

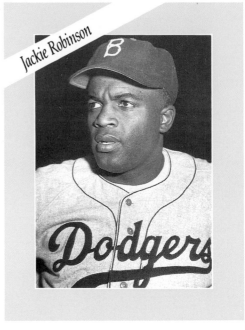

Hank Greenberg

Jackie Robinson

LEFT: Manager Connie Mack

RIGHT: Ralph Kiner

Harry Hooper	OF	1909–1925	1971
Rogers Hornsby	2B	1915–1937	1942
Waite Hoyt	P	1918–1938	1969
Carl Hubbell	P	1928–1943	1947
Catfish Hunter	P	1965–1979	1987
Monte Irvin*	OF	1949–1956	1973
Travis Jackson	SS	1922–1936	1982
Hugh Jennings	SS	1891–1918	1945
Judy Johnson*	3B		1975
Walter Johnson	P	1907–1927	1936
Addie Joss	P	1902–1910	1978
Al Kaline	OF	1953–1974	1980
Tim Keefe	P	1880–1893	1964
Willie Keeler	OF	1892–1910	1939
George Kell	3B	1943–1957	1983
Joe Kelley	OF	1891–1908	1971
George Kelly	1B	1915–1932	1973
King Kelly	C	1878–1893	1945
Harmon Killebrew	1B–3B	1954–1975	1984
Ralph Kiner	OF	1946–1955	1975
Chuck Klein	OF	1928–1944	1979
Sandy Koufax	P	1955–1966	1971
Nap Lajoie	2B	1896–1916	1937
Bob Lemon	P	1941–1958	1976
Buck Leonard*	1B		1972
Fred Lindstrom	3B	1924–1936	1976
John Henry Lloyd*	SS–1B		1976
Ernie Lombardi	C	1931–1947	1986
Ted Lyons	P	1923–1946	1955
Mickey Mantle	OF	1951–1968	1974
Heinie Manush	OF	1923–1939	1964
Rabbit Maranville	SS–2B	1912–1935	1954
Juan Marichal	P	1960–1975	1983
Rube Marquard	P	1908–1925	1971
Eddie Mathews	3B	1952–1968	1978
Christy Mathewson	P	1900–1916	1936
Willie Mays	OF	1951–1973	1979
Tommy McCarthy	OF	1884–1896	1946
Willie McCovey	1B	1959–1980	1986
Joe McGinnity	P	1899–1908	1946
Joe Medwick	OF	1932–1948	1968

Johnny Mize	1B	1936–1953	1981
Stan Musial	OF–1B	1941–1963	1969
Kid Nichols	P	1890–1906	1949
Jim O'Rourke	OF	1876–1904	1945
Mel Ott	OF	1926–1947	1951
Satchel Paige*	P	1948–1965	1971
Herb Pennock	P	1912–1934	1948
Eddie Plank	P	1901–1917	1946
Hoss Radbourn	P	1880–1891	1939
Pee Wee Reese	SS	1940–1958	1984
Sam Rice	OF	1915–1935	1963
Eppa Rixey	P	1912–1933	1963
Robin Roberts	P	1948–1966	1976
Brooks Robinson	3B	1955–1977	1983
Frank Robinson	OF	1956–1976	1982
Jackie Robinson	2B	1947–1956	1962
Edd Roush	OF	1913–1931	1962
Red Ruffing	P	1924–1947	1967
Amos Rusie	P	1889–1901	1977
Babe Ruth	OF	1914–1935	1936
Ray Schalk	C	1912–1929	1955
Joe Sewell	SS	1920–1933	1977
Al Simmons	OF	1924–1944	1953
George Sisler	1B	1915–1930	1939
Enos Slaughter	OF	1938–1959	1985
Duke Snider	OF	1947–1964	1980
Warren Spahn	P	1942–1965	1973
Al Spalding	P	1871–1878	1939
Tris Speaker	OF	1907–1928	1937
Bill Terry	1B	1923–1936	1954
Sam Thompson	OF	1885–1906	1974
Joe Tinker	SS	1902–1916	1946
Pie Traynor	3B	1920–1937	1948
Dazzy Vance	P	1915–1935	1955
Arky Vaughn	SS–OF	1932–1948	1985
Rube Waddell	P	1897–1910	1946
Honus Wagner	SS	1897–1917	1936
Bobby Wallace	SS	1894–1918	1953
Ed Walsh	P	1904–1917	1946
Lloyd Waner	OF	1927–1945	1967
Paul Waner	OF	1926–1945	1952

BELOW: Mickey Cochrane

Monte Ward	2B–P	1878–1894	1964
Mickey Welch	P	1880–1892	1973
Zach Wheat	OF	1909–1927	1959
Hoyt Wilhelm	P	1952–1972	1985
Billy Williams	OF	1959–1976	1987
Ted Williams	OF	1939–1960	1966
Hack Wilson	OF	1923–1934	1979
Early Wynn	P	1939–1963	1971
Cy Young	P	1890–1911	1937
Ross Youngs	OF	1917–1926	1972

MANAGERS	YEAR SELECTED
Walt Alston	1983
Charles Comiskey	1939
Clark Griffith	1946
Bucky Harris	1974
Miller Huggins	1964
Al Lopez	1977
Connie Mack	1937
Joe McCarthy	1957
John McGraw	1937
Bill McKechnie	1962
Wilbert Robinson	1945
Casey Stengel	1974
Harry Wright	1953
George Wright	1937

SELECTED FOR MERITORIOUS SERVICE	
Edward Barrow	(Manager-Executive)
Morgan G. Bulkeley	(Executive)
Alexander J. Cartwright	(Executive)
Henry Chadwick	(Writer-Statistician)
John "Jocko" Conlan	(Umpire)
Thomas Connolly	(Umpire)
William G. Evans	(Umpire-Executive)
Andrew "Rube" Foster	(Player-Executive)
Ford C. Frick	(Commissioner-Executive)
William Harridge	(Executive)
Cal Hubbard	(Umpire)
B. Bancroft Johnson	(Executive)
William Klem	(Umpire)
Kenesaw M. Landis	(Commissioner)
Larry S. MacPhail	(Executive)
W. Branch Rickey	(Manager-Executive)
George M. Weiss	(Executive)

Index

Numbers in *italics* refer to pictures